HOME-BASED BUSINESS SERIES

D0128111

How to Start a Home-Based
Interior Design Business

Third Edition

Suzanne DeWalt

The
Globe
Pequot
Press

Text design by Mary Ballachino

ISBN: 0-7627-2481-1
ISSN: 1546-3346

Manufactured in the United States of America
Third Edition/Second Printing

To Jeremy, my Inspiration

Contents

Acknowledgments

I have been blessed in my life. I'm surrounded by people who support me and believe in me and my dreams. They are:

Cheetah, who has been my writing partner from the beginning, and who was thoughtful enough not to walk across the keyboard during the important parts . . .

My editor, Laura Strom, for having the courage to hire an unknown writer and the patience to work with one. Laura, you've made it easier than it ought to be . . .

My parents, Ed and Peggy Kearns, who have managed to instill a belief in me that I could do anything. I hope Jeremy grows up to love and respect me as much as I do you.

Introduction

Some people are just born lucky. I started my interior design business in the depths of the recession in Texas. The oil business was steadily falling, and the real estate market had just crashed. Against all advice, I quit my secure job as a manufacturers' representative and opened my business. I did everything wrong. I didn't have a business plan, I paid full price for all of my sample books, and I accepted whatever discounts the manufacturers gave me. I combed the bookstores looking for information that would tell me how to run an interior design business. I couldn't even find one book.

I got most of my information by talking to the manufacturers' representatives and contractors. I took on my first fabric line simply because the sales representative happened to be in the drapery workroom at the same time I was. I got most of my business advice from my father and listened diligently to my mother's suggestions on color and design.

Amazingly, through trial and error, I went on to build a successful business. Within six years I had five designers working for me, and I eventually hired a sales manager. I was soon working for builders, doing new homeowner color selections, and designing model homes.

I feel that if I'd had a blueprint of some sort I might have had an easier start and not made so many mistakes along the way. My journey would have been easier. I hope to give you that advantage with this book. In it I describe exactly what you can expect when starting an interior design business, and I'll keep you from making mistakes by educating you about the business and how it works. I'll not only teach you the business aspect of interior design but will provide you with all of the elusive formulas and charts that new designers have such a hard time finding. In short, I hope to make your journey easier than mine. So, get comfortable, sharpen your pencils, and let's get started on making your dream a reality!

Chapter One
Design 101

Does your heart skip a beat when colors blend together perfectly? Does the concept of combining patterns excite you? Does the idea of spending other people's money make you want to do back flips? If you answered yes to these questions, you may have the beginnings of what it takes to become a great interior designer.

Of course, there is more to this business than designing throw pillows and rearranging furniture. There is the business aspect. You can be the most gifted, talented, and creative person in the world, but if you don't run your business wisely, you will not make it in this competitive field. In this book I provide information that will help you set up and run a successful home-based interior design business. In addition to this information, you will learn the basics of interior design. You'll have formulas and charts at your fingertips which will provide relevant information so that you can get started in this fun and profitable business.

The design business is a natural home-based business. Most of the sales take place in the customer's home because of the need to match color swatches to existing furniture or measure the windows for draperies. It is rare that a customer will ever have the need to come to your office. Of course, there are exceptions. As your business expands you may want to consider adding builders to your list of clientele, and some may require that you have an office. (More about this later.)

The other good news about the design business is that it will always be in demand. People will always buy new homes or remodel their old ones. In addition to that, the fact that this business can be started anywhere adds to the appeal. Every large city has dozens of design companies, and every small town has at least one or two. The design companies that market themselves as product-driven companies have an even greater advantage. For example, when a person moves into a new home, he or she may not be able to afford a "designer" but will definitely need new window coverings and maybe carpet, or perhaps have a sofa that needs to be reupholstered. I will explain the various marketing techniques for this type of business in the advertising chapter.

What Are Your Options?

The design field is multifaceted. There are many types of designers, each doing a very different and specific job. Your first step will be to determine what type of designer you want to be. First, let's define the differences between a decorator and a designer.

- A *decorator* is usually what you call yourself when just starting out in business. You have the same responsibilities as a designer, but not the title. Clients will still rely on you for help with the design of their home. Just as a designer, you will be responsible for the ordering and installation of the products.
- A *designer* is a decorator who is certified by the American Society of Interior Designers (ASID). To achieve ASID certification, you must have worked in the field for a number of years and then pass an exam. Anyone who has not passed this exam may not use the title of designer; instead, the person is called a decorator. A decorator is just as well received in the public eye as a designer is. This change has come about recently, and quite frankly, the only people who know the difference between a designer and a decorator are the people working in the field. For simplicity, I will use the title of designer throughout this book.

The two basic types of designers are product-driven designers and consultation-only designers. Both types work in both residential and commercial markets. Your first step in opening a design business is to determine what type and market you would best be suited for. The following questions may help you decide.

1. Are you self-motivated? If a drapery is hanging wrong, would you climb a ladder and straighten it out or would you call an installer to do it for you? If you would

climb the ladder yourself, you would do well as a hands-on, product-driven designer.

2. Do you enjoy working in homes, or do you prefer the corporate atmosphere? Obviously, if you prefer working with people in their homes, you would enjoy working as a residential designer, but if you thrive in the corporate atmosphere, you would be better suited as a commercial designer.

3. Are you good with math? Can you use a tape measure? You must be good with math and a tape measure to be successful as a product-driven designer. This quality applies to both the residential and commercial fields.

4. Are you good at follow-through? All the types of designers must exhibit proper follow-through to be successful; however, when working as a consultation-only designer, your relationship with the client is short-lived, so follow-through isn't as important.

5. How well do you handle conflict? The ability to handle it well is a must for all types of designers but most important for product-driven designers.

6. If a client called you to buy just one vertical blind for her new home, would you consider taking the job? If you consider small jobs a gateway to larger ones, you will do well as a product-driven designer.

7. Are you a self-learner? Can you read a book or an article about a product and feel confident enough to sell it? Again, this is an important trait for a residential or commercial product-driven designer.

Product-Driven Designer

If you would climb up a ladder to straighten a drapery, can handle a tape measure (the most important tool a designer carries), and can deal with an emotional client, you are probably best suited as a hands-on, residential or commercial product-driven designer. This is the best role for a new designer to take when just starting out in business. It is usually the most profitable for the new designer because there are a wide variety of products to be sold. You are marketing the products more than the design services in this type of business. We've all seen ads for window covering, flooring, and wallpaper companies. These are usually owned by designers who are trying to appeal to a broader customer base. There are plenty of design jobs to be had by a product-driven design business, but a large portion of its cash flow is dependent on product sales alone.

In this type of business, the designer usually advertises various products and offers free design advice if the client purchases all the products from her or him. There is a generous markup on most of the products, so it is well worth your time. Most designers limit the time spent in the customer's home with a prearranged agreement and charge a per hour fee if the customer requires more time (depending on how large the product sale is). Another way to make sure you do not waste your time is to let your customers know that if they buy the product from someone else after you have spent time with them, they will be billed a predetermined hourly design fee.

Design Consultant

Your other option is to market yourself as a design consultant, or a consultation-only designer. This is usually done after a designer has been in business for a number of years and has built up a reputation and a list of references. An interior design degree is necessary in this type of situation. When you get to this stage of your career, you can charge a hefty fee by simply giving advice about the design of a room or an office. It is more difficult to succeed in this business because you are not selling any products, just your expertise. Before you can call yourself a design consultant, you should have quite a few years of experience working in the field. An option for those who want to have this type of business is to spend a number of years working at a high-end furniture store or an upscale design shop gaining experience.

Residential or Commercial?

Once you've decided whether to be a product-driven designer or a design consultant, the other choice you will have to make is whether you want to work in the residential or the commercial market. It is entirely possible and likely that you will perform jobs in both the residential and commercial fields, but you need to decide which you want to target more aggressively. If you decide to cater to residential clients, you will surely design the homes of business owners and managers, which will lead to commercial jobs. On the other hand, if you decide that you prefer the corporate atmosphere, the department heads and managers all have homes that may require your services.

Generally, residential jobs are smaller in size but reap a higher profit margin. You are working directly with the homeowner, and many close relationships and even friendships are formed this way. You will be working with small details, such as designing place mats to coordinate with the kitchen valance you've just hung.

Commercial jobs are usually not that intimate. The retail prices of the jobs are higher, but there is a substantially lower profit margin. If you are designing the bedspreads and draperies for a hotel, more than likely the rooms will all look the same, so after choosing the fabric, it's just a matter of taking measurements and working up a bid.

I'm going to assume, for the purpose of this book, that most of you will be interested in becoming a product-driven designer working in either the residential or commercial field.

Working with Builders

Another source of income for any type of designer is builder accounts. The product-driven residential designer is the most likely candidate for this type of business because he or she will already have the necessary manufacturer accounts set up. This designer will have the various sample books and pricing structures needed to work with a builder.

There are two ways that working with builders can bring you business: (1) model home design and (2) new homeowner color selections. A builder usually wants a track record from a designer before assigning this type of work, but there are exceptions. I was lucky in my business; I landed one of these accounts within the first three years of business. I accomplished this with much persistence (I bugged them so much that they finally said yes just to shut me up) and hard work, so it is possible. I will briefly describe the ins and outs of this type of work.

1. *Model home design.* There is not a lot of money to be made decorating models, but indirectly it can pay well. A builder sets aside a decorating budget for each model home that he or she builds. It is almost always not enough, and the designer ends up having to persuade (beg) furniture stores to lend pieces to furnish

the house. This is a time-consuming affair, and even though the designer is paid minimally for these efforts, she or he is expected to attend countless meetings and walk-throughs with the builder. Yet the competition for model home design work is fierce. There is a fair amount of recognition that stems from decorating a model (your company name will be posted on signs throughout the house). The big payoff from this type of work is the opportunity to do the color selection work for the builder. Do not accept model home work without a promise from the builder to give you that business.

2. *Color selections.* When people buy a new home, they must pick out carpet, vinyl, wallpaper, brick, indoor and outdoor paint, appliance colors, tile, and a roof. The builder usually hires a designer to help the customer with these decisions. The builder then pays the designer per color selection, generally $150 to $250. In addition to the color selection fee, the designer has the first shot at getting the customer's business for window coverings, furniture, or design consulting business. As the designer, you have a great opportunity to build a rapport with the customer, so you should at least get a chance to bid on the job. An average builder sells ten to twenty houses per month, so you can imagine the sales opportunities that exist. (I can hear the more industrious of you pounding away at a calculator as you read.) Some builders will require that you have a showroom to do color selections, but more and more builders are setting aside a room in one of their model homes for the process. It won't hurt for you to make the suggestion to builders; maybe they just haven't thought of it yet themselves.

What Does a Designer Do?

Webster's Collegiate Dictionary defines *designer* as "one who specializes in interior design." Webster needs to spend some time with today's interior designer. It's true, an interior designer does design, but there are many other tasks involved in the running of a design business. This book will cover all of the areas in detail, but here is a basic job description:

- You will be responsible for marketing your company. This will include designing all the layouts for your advertising as well as deciding where to advertise. This also will include calling on real estate agents and architects and asking for business. (See chapter 6 for more detail.) You will also have to cold-call residential and commercial customers.

- You will be the scheduler and rescheduler for all of your design appointments. You will also have to run several work crews, including but not limited to window covering installers, carpet layers, wallpaper hangers, and carpenters.
- You will have to be patient and listen to your client's needs. You will have to search through countless sample books to find the combination to satisfy your customer's dreams. There will be times when you will have to work up numerous presentations until you find the one that your client likes enough to buy.
- You will have to be a salesperson in every sense of the word. Not only will you have to be talented in design, you also will have to be able to convey your ideas to customers in a way that will make them want to buy.
- You will be responsible for mapping out a room, taking measurements for draperies or flooring, and sometimes (in a pinch) even doing simple installations. This means you must be knowledgeable in every aspect of the business, not only design.
- You will have to work up bids on each job and estimate the materials needed for each product.
- You will have to order all the materials needed for a job from each manufacturer (this is where a fax machine or e-mail account comes in handy) and then take responsibility if there is too much or too little.
- You will have to log in each product and then check it for flaws, missing parts, and color variations.
- You will have to collect the deposits and balances from each of your customers. You also will be the bill collector in the event that one of your clients refuses to pay. In addition to the small aspects of bookkeeping, you will be responsible for the overall record keeping of your business, including taxes.
- You sometimes will be dealing with irate and unsatisfied customers, one of the most frustrating aspects of this job. Since yours is a custom business, it is inevitable that you will have some problems. For instance, you may be manufacturing a pair of custom draperies for a client's home, and it is important to the

client that the draperies are installed by Christmas, which is five weeks away—just enough time to get the job done. When you place the order, you verify that there is enough fabric in stock to complete the job. You put the file away and wait for the draperies to arrive. Two and a half weeks later, you receive a postcard in the mail from the manufacturer explaining that there was a flaw in the fabric and the new fabric has been ordered from the mill; your new delivery date for the goods is January 15. It will be your responsibility to call your customer and explain that not only will the draperies not be ready in time for the holidays, but it's now too late to choose another fabric. The customer will not care that it's not your fault. If you have a problem dealing with situations like this, you might want to rethink your decision of becoming a designer, because such glitches are not uncommon.

- You also will act as a delivery person. It will be your responsibility to make sure the fabric gets to the workroom, the wallpaper gets to the right house, or your vacationing client's home is open for the work crews on a Saturday or Sunday.
- You will have to learn how to budget your time with each customer to avoid turning a sales call into a social hour. At times, you will be looked upon as a friend, confidant, and even marriage counselor.
- You will have to negotiate with the sales representatives for better discounts on products. You will be constantly bombarded with new products, and you will have to decide what you will and will not sell in your business.
- You will have to find the time to keep all the products updated. Things change fast in this business, and if you sell a product that has been discontinued, it will be embarrassing to explain to your client that you had not gotten around to updating your samples.
- You will be responsible for creating and updating your Web site, including product offerings, pricing structures, and all other content. In addition, you will have to create and implement the Internet marketing plan.

Required Traits for the Job

While the world of interior design is a challenging, fulfilling career, it takes a unique individual to rise to the challenges that are encountered every day in this job. Here are some important traits that help in running a successful home-based interior design business. Be honest with yourself as you read through them, because every one of them is vitally important to this career.

- *Self-esteem.* You will run into many obstacles, especially when just starting your business. Real estate agents will tell you no, you will lose bids to competitors, and customers will be disappointed with your work. It's essential to have an attitude that will allow you to dust yourself off after disappointments and keep going.
- *A good support group.* If you are married, it's important that your spouse (and children, if you have them) back up your decision to go into business for yourself. There will be evenings when you work all night to meet a deadline and if you don't get support, it will be hard to keep motivated. If you are not married and don't have children, make sure your friends and family are aware that at times you will need their support and understanding.
- *Patience.* As a designer, you will come across many situations that test your patience. A customer will remember a fabric being just a shade bluer, or someone will take up hours of your time, probing your mind for ideas, then decide not to buy anything. Such aggravation is just part of the job.
- *Organization.* Because of the many details you will be handling at any given moment, organization is key. You will probably have three or four jobs (maybe more) going on at one time, and you must keep track of the progress of all of them.
- *Motivation.* Your alarm clock will be your only boss in the morning. No one will tell you to go out and market your business or to be on time to your appointment. You must be a self-starter and self-disciplined in order to be successful in a home-based business.
- *The ability to listen.* To be a good designer and salesperson, you must be able to listen to the client's needs; only then can you fill them. For example, some customers already know exactly what they want and are just looking for someone to

confirm their ideas. These are special cases, and you will have to listen carefully to what they say in order to respond appropriately.

- *Authoritativeness.* A designer will be in charge of all aspects of a job, including the installation. You will have to supervise numerous workers during the course of the day. There will be times when your drapery installer has a different vision than yours about the way a pair of draperies needs to be hung, and you will have to make the authoritative decision.
- *Stable personality.* This business is filled with many ups and downs, and they can all occur on the same day. A steady temperament will help you deal with the crises and successes better.
- *Interest in people.* Regardless of whether you deal in residential or commercial jobs, you will be in constant contact with people. Some will change their minds on a continual basis and call you ten times a day. This is all part of the job, so if you don't like people—that is, if you aren't a "people person"—then this may not be the career for you.
- *Mathematical ability.* Although advanced math skills are not mandatory, the basics are. Almost every product you sell will require the use of a tape measure and some basic arithmetic calculations.

The Myths and Realities of Entrepreneurship

Before we discuss the details of setting up your business, let's examine your motives for wanting to be self-employed. You have your own reasons for wanting to be your own boss, as does everyone else who wants to try it, so I would like to clear up some of the misconceptions that are associated with self-employment.

MYTH: No one tells you what to do; you are your own boss.

REALITY: Every one of your customers will be your boss. Remember the old adage that says the customer is always right? When operating a small business, that is the golden rule. Word of mouth or referral business is absolutely the best business you can get. If you have an unhappy customer, you would be surprised how fast word will spread around the neighborhood (and among that person's coworkers, friends, family, etc.). On the other hand, a satisfied customer can be an inexpensive, productive form of advertising.

MYTH: Your time will be your own.

REALITY: There is no one to pass your work on to when you're tired or have other plans. To use an old cliché, the buck stops with you. If you have a proposal to work up on the weekend of a family campout, you have to make a choice. The work fairy is not going to do it for you while you're out grilling hot dogs.

MYTH: You will become instantly rich.

REALITY: While it is possible to make an excellent income running your own business, it will not happen overnight. Some businesses take years to even turn a profit. This business is better than most because of the low start-up cost and the ability to run it out of your home, but don't expect to become a millionaire overnight. This business, as all businesses, takes hard work in order to be successful.

MYTH: You won't have to work as hard as you do when working for someone else.

REALITY: Because you are the only one responsible for your business, you will have to work twice or three times as hard as you would have working a 9-to-5 job. You may only have to go on two appointments a day to make your required income, but there is much to be done besides selling the product. If this is one of your misconceptions (as it was one of mine, and boy, was *I* in for a surprise!), please refer back to the basic job description.

A Few Loose Ends

I would like to make a few recommendations for things that you can do before you start your own business. Most people jump right in, as I did, and the road to success inevitably becomes harder than it has to be. You are taking the first positive step by reading this book, but to ensure your success, I have a few other suggestions. These suggestions assume that you are still employed by someone other than yourself. There are many advantages of being employed when you make the decision to go into business for yourself. You will be in a better position than those who aren't employed because you can take advantage of your situation to make things go easier once you are out on your own. Here are a few hints:

1. If you can save three (preferably six) months of living expenses, you will be way ahead of the game. If you have the time (or patience), start saving long before you plan to open the doors of your new business; that may eliminate the need to apply for a small business loan.

2. If you need a car, buy one while you still have a paycheck. Most financial institutions will loan you money more readily if you have a steady paycheck coming in.

3. If you have health insurance, plan to continue it through the Consolidated Omnibus Budget Reconciliation Act. You will have to pay the entire premium up front, plus a fee. If this is not in your budget, sign up for basic health insurance while you're still covered under your existing policy. Do the same thing with your life insurance policy.

4. If you own your home, consider opening a home-equity line of credit as an alternative source of financing. Bankers will be more cooperative about loans if you are still employed.

Testing the Waters

So you love the thought of interior design. Perhaps, even after reading this far in the book, you are still enchanted with the idea. Then test it. This may be the hardest suggestion to swallow, but it's also one of the most important. Even a person who has been in the design field for ten years doesn't know everything about this business—it's just impossible. To further your chances of success, you should spend a little time working for an established design firm. It will enable you to get to know the areas of town that offer the most business, and that in turn will tell you where to concentrate your marketing efforts. It also will give you a chance to work with and become comfortable with the different products and manufacturers. This experience will give you practical knowledge in the design field. When first starting out in this complicated business, you are sure to make costly mistakes. Being employed and trained by someone else will soften the blow on your pocketbook throughout the learning curve. Make sure that you train with a company that does not require you to sign a noncompete agreement (see chapter 10 for further explanation) as part of your employment.

Determining Your Level of Participation

This business can be run on a part-time or full-time basis, depending on how much time you want to devote to it. Obviously, the more you work, the more money you will make. Even part-time interior design is a time-consuming business. If you decide to go into it full time, be prepared to work a minimum of ten to twelve hours a day in the beginning. You will have more flexibility than most jobs. Because you are in control of your schedule, you can pencil in a dentist appointment without having to ask anyone.

If You Have Children

Ask any parent what they want more of, and the answer you'll likely get is time. So how can a parent of a small child possibly run a business out of his or her home? The answer is simple: structure and planning. You may have to get up earlier in the morning to figure a bid or stay up late at night to go through fabric swatches for that picky customer, but if you are willing to schedule your day, and stick to it, you should be able to squeeze out a few more hours in the day. For example, when my son was younger, I made sure that he went to the park every day before nap time so that he'd be exhausted from play and likelier to sleep longer.

If your spouse is willing to help, you can schedule your appointments in the evenings and on the weekends, which is when most of your clients will want to meet with you anyway. Paperwork and phone orders can be taken care of in the day, during nap time, for instance.

Day care is another option, either limited or on a full-time basis. If you're uncomfortable with leaving your child at a day care facility, consider bringing a baby-sitter into your home. By closing yourself up in your office with a "disturb only in an emergency" mentality, you can be quite productive. Don't forget about any nearby relatives—they can be invaluable in a deadline situation.

Be sure to include your children in your work, rather than excluding them. If they know that work time is fun because they get to do "paperwork" or open mail, they won't resist or automatically demand attention every time you sit down to work.

Read, Read, Read

There are quite a few informative trade magazines that offer a wealth of information. In addition to interior design magazines, there are specific ones dealing with products such as window coverings, carpet, wood flooring, and more. It is to your advantage to subscribe to and read these periodicals on a monthly basis. They will keep you updated on new products and will give you ideas about how to make use of the existing ones. I have provided a list of the trade magazines in the appendix of this book.

Associations

There are a number of associations connected to the design field that will increase your knowledge as well as give you possible leads for your business. Some of the associations you may want to look into are:

- *The Builders Association*
  This is an organization that consists of builders working in a particular area. They usually put on events, such as the Parade of Homes, and require the services of interior designers frequently. This is also a good place to meet business contacts for model home jobs and new homeowner color selections. Builders Association chapters usually hold meetings and have social functions. There is a yearly fee required to join; check with your local association for specific information.

- *The Board of Realtors*
  This organization is made up of real estate agents who also have a constant need for interior designers. For example, when an agent is representing a client who is selling a home, they may need new carpet or window coverings to make the home more marketable. That's where you come in. The agent has to feel confident in her recommendation, and once you build a relationship with her by doing a few quality jobs, the referrals will start coming with more frequency. The key to this association is to network, pass out your cards, and ask for business. If you do quality work at reasonable prices, the word will get around. There is also a nominal fee involved for joining this group. Once again, check with the group in your local area for specifics.

- *Various Apartment Associations*
  The owners and managers of all apartment complexes must buy blinds, carpet, and wallpaper. While this part of the business is extremely competitive, the model apartments and offices are not. Make contacts with the key people in the organizations and ask for a chance to bid on their upcoming jobs.

- *Chambers of Commerce, Small Business Associations, and Countless Others*
  The more associations you join, the more networking you will do, and the more business you will gain. The wonderful thing about this business is that everyone, at one time or another, will need your services. I recommend joining as many associations as you have time for. It's a great way to market your business. The appendix includes a selection of associations. Look in your local yellow pages under "Associations" for a complete listing.

Further Your Education

It's not a bad idea, in addition to your reading, to take a few courses. With the number of people improving their lives through education, there are countless courses offered at night and on the weekends. There are some interior design degrees that only require one year of study. Some other courses you might consider are accounting, tax courses, marketing, and basic business classes. In addition to these, there are seminars put on by manufacturers specifically designed for this business, such as how-tos for the various products, installation guidelines, and tips for up-selling to more expensive products.

Summary

If this chapter has taught you anything, it is to be prepared before opening your business. When taking the leap from working for someone else to being your own boss, your road to success will be much less bumpy if you are prepared. Be realistic with yourself, and if you know of an area that you're weak in, work on it. Remember, the more you can plan while still on someone else's payroll, the better off you will be when you take that final, exciting step toward your new independent lifestyle.

Chapter Two

Setting Up Shop

Among the many benefits of running a business from your home is that your office will be located approximately one minute from your bedroom. This can work either for or against you. You must be self-motivated to work out of your home because the distractions will be numerous: your children will want your full attention, your spouse will expect you to run errands in your "spare time," your friends will call daily wanting to gossip, the remote control will entice you, and your house will probably never be cleaner. (Giving in to such distractions is commonly known as a procrastination technique in this business.) If you are a self-motivated person, as I suspect you are if you are still reading, you can overcome these obstacles. The first thing you must do is set up your work space. It needs to be an area that is dedicated solely to your business. When you walk into this space, whether it's an entire room or a partitioned-off section of a larger room (i.e., the living room), you are at work. This concept needs to be understood by your family members, friends, and, most importantly, you.

Interior design is a business of details, and you must be equipped to handle them. It would be ideal if you have an extra study or a bedroom that you can convert into an office, but if not, a partitioned section of your living room, kitchen, or garage will do for starters. You need to take into consideration your individual needs. If you have special requirements like children or other responsibilities, you need to keep that in mind when determining your office needs. Peace and quiet is something that should be considered when choosing your office space, so be sure to consider the noise level of the area as well as the traffic volume. You will be working on complicated bids that take a tremendous amount of concentration.

What You'll Need

The items you need in your office are basic. Some people make the mistake of going to the office supply store and spending a bundle; there is no need to. When first opening a business, you just need the basics. Use the bulk of your start-up capital for more important things, such as samples and advertising. (The projected start-up cost worksheet in chapter 3 will help you plan more effectively.)

Here is a list of necessities:

- *Desk, filing cabinet, and storage cabinet* (to be used for all of your forms and miscellaneous office supplies). You can usually find these at a secondhand store or a discount office store reasonably priced.
- *Basic office supplies.* This includes paper, pens, paper clips, standard and expandable file folders, a Rolodex, message pads, calculators (desktop and portable), and a briefcase (to be used on your appointments). Again, these items can be bought at a discount office supply store.
- *Computer.* A computer is essential in today's technological environment. With it you can keep track of your jobs, estimate jobs, stay on top of balances due, and perform your overall bookkeeping. You can save money by looking for a model that includes fax capabilities and a scanner. If it's not in your budget at first, work toward buying one as soon as possible.
- *Phone with an answering machine or an answering service.* I highly recommend a second phone line dedicated entirely to your business. When you answer your business phone, you should answer in a professional manner, stating the name of your business. The problem with using a home line is that a child may answer or a client may call at an inopportune time, costing you business. A good phone with two or three incoming lines is best. When customers call and continuously get a busy signal, they may give up and call somebody else. An answering machine can also be a hindrance. Some people have a problem leaving a message on a machine. If you do decide to use one, make sure you buy one that will allow you to pick up your messages throughout the day. Returning phone calls promptly can make the difference between a $10 or a $10,000 day. Another great option is

to buy a phone with a distinctive ring feature. This will allow you to differentiate between business and personal calls.

A good answering service can be a great benefit to your business. When searching for a service to do business with, ask for referrals and call them. Then call the companies at a time when the service is answering for them; this will tell you everything you need to know about the company.

- *Cellular phone.* Nowadays, most businesspeople must be readily available. By carrying a cellular phone, and printing the number on your business cards, you'll ensure that your customers can always find you.

- *Fax machine.* This item will become increasingly important as your business grows. It's a real time-saver when placing orders. Sometimes, depending on the number of orders you have to place, it can take up to an hour to call them in. If you are dealing with commercial bids, a fax machine is a must. Commercial clients expect to fax you information and for you to promptly send back a reply. There will be times when even a residential customer will ask that a bid be faxed to her or him. If you decide to buy a fax machine, make sure you buy one with a copy option. You will make a lot of copies in this business and will eventually need a copier, but a fax copier is fine in the beginning. Look for a combo machine that offers fax, printer, and scanner in one. This will not only save you space, but as of this writing, you can pick one up for under $200.

- *Forms and documents.* We will go into more detail on these later; but for now know that they are numerous. You will need a place to store them, such as a filing cabinet.

- *Tape measure.* This item deserves a paragraph for itself. If you do not know how to use and read a tape measure, start practicing now. You will need to take measurements for everything that you sell. Most of the items measured will be taken to ⅛ inch. (More about this in chapter 9.)

- *Business cards, letterhead, envelopes, and postage.* These things are all wise investments for any business. When you send out correspondence, you will want to project a professional image, and you will need business cards in many situations. These are a form of advertising for your company and should be the best you can afford.

- *Camera.* You will want to start a portfolio that includes your best jobs as soon as you can. Some customers will request to see your portfolio before doing business with you. Use color film and try to make the focal point of each picture your work that you want displayed. Until you are able to put together a portfolio with pictures of your jobs, use magazine pictures that reflect your style. As you get more and more of your own pictures, replace the magazine pictures with them, and before long you will have a professional portfolio. If you plan on creating a Web site or advertising on the Internet, you might consider getting a digital camera. Then you can take pictures of your designs and post them on your site.

Vertically Challenged

Not everyone is fortunate enough to have an entire room to dedicate to a home office; many have to share space with another part of the house. In these instances, it's important to make good use of vertical wall space in lieu of horizontal floor space. Here are a few hints that will help you make the best possible use of your limited space.

- Make use of your existing furniture. In the beginning, it may make sense to share the family desk or use half of the bookshelves for your business books and files. This will not only save space, it will keep your start-up costs to a minimum.
- Buy special-needs office equipment. There are desks on the market that will satisfy every space challenge. Look into rollaway desks (desks on wheels that can be rolled into a closet at the end of the workday); self-contained offices, which include everything you need, including a chair, which tucks into a cabinet when not in use; and rolltop desks, which will complement almost any room.
- Buy combination office equipment. Why buy a fax machine, printer, and scanner when you can get it all in one machine? Not only will you save space, it will be easier on your pocketbook as well.

Storage Space

Another area important to your business is the storage space needed for your samples. Among the samples you will have to inventory are fabric for draperies and upholstery, miniblinds, vertical blinds, shutters, wallpaper, carpet and other flooring, bedding, and paint, just to name a few. If your office is large enough, you can set up your samples on a wall with one of the various sample rack systems available. One of the easiest and least expensive ways to do so is with Peg-Board. Panel your wall with it, leaving enough space to use S-hooks to hang your samples. Combine this system with a few shelves and you will be able to fit a large amount of samples in a small space. Some of your sales representatives will try to sell you the costly racks that have been designed for their samples, but unless you are in a showroom setting, they are not worth the money. Remember, no one will see them but you.

Off-Site Storage Space

You will also need a space for incoming products. Some of the products, such as long vertical blinds or carpet rolls, can be quite large and require a lot of storage space. Most of the carpet delivery companies will not deliver a roll of carpet unless there is a forklift on the premises. Have you ever tried lifting a roll of carpet by yourself? Since manually lifting the carpet is out of the question, you will need to find a place that has a forklift you can use. The best solution is a local freight company. Call some companies (you can find the listing under "Freight Companies" in your local yellow pages) and explain that you need to hire them to receive your carpet purchases. They will give you their guidelines and explain their rates to you. Choose one, then simply list the freight company's address on the order form when ordering the carpet, and it will be delivered to that address. Your carpet installer will pick it up there. The freight company will charge you a predetermined fee on each delivery that will have to be paid before the carpet is picked up.

Your garage or storage shed will serve your purposes for the rest of your deliveries. Make sure that your storage space will stay dry in bad weather, because you will be receiving fabrics and other delicate goods.

You will also have UPS and other delivery companies knocking at your door daily. Build a rapport with the drivers, so that they will leave the delivery in the appropriate place and not out in the rain or snow when you're not at home.

Your Car

You will have a second office while operating your new business—your car. Between running to and from appointments and marketing your business, most of your time will be spent in your office-away-from-your-office. Because of this, I recommend that you drive a car that has a large trunk space and is comfortable. A minivan is used frequently in this business because it's easy to keep your samples and paperwork organized. Of course, there are exceptions to this rule. (When I first started my business I drove a Volkswagen Cabriolet convertible. It was cramped and unorganized most of the time, which made my job harder. I eventually sold it and bought a bigger car.)

You will carry with you the samples that you tend to use the most, along with the price lists that go with them. This will eliminate the need to lug them to and from your office daily. Business cards, tape measure, portable calculator, invoices, and notebook will also be carried in your car. There will be times when you are marketing in a neighborhood and a homeowner will ask you to come in and give an on-the-spot estimate.

It's hard to keep your car efficient and organized without a system. I suggest you set up boxes in the trunk and put the samples in them, arranging them according to the frequency of use. Another box in the backseat will hold the price lists, invoices, and other paperwork. In addition to that, your briefcase that you carry with you at all times will hold your business cards, pens, calculator, tape measure, and duplicates of any forms you might need. It sounds like a lot of preplanning and backup, but it's necessary in order to make you appear professional. I can't tell you how many times I have won bids from competitors whose clients lost faith in them because they were messy and unorganized. Always present yourself as a professional and you will be that much ahead of your competition.

A Word about Your Appearance

I have heard two schools of thought on this subject. The first is that since you own your business, you can dress however you want. This is true—to an extent. Let me illustrate with a true story. A few years back when suits were in style that used shorts instead of skirts, I was ecstatic. I lived in a hot and humid climate, and I thought these new suits were the answer to my prayers. I promptly went out and bought five or six of them and then proceeded to wear them on my appointments. My sales dropped drastically! They were just too casual for a professional appointment. Clients look at the way you are dressed as part of the overall picture of you as a designer. After all, if you can't dress yourself, or are inappropriately dressed, how are you going to put their house together?

The second school of thought says that you should dress up for work. Yet one thing I have seen new designers do is overdress. This is commonly thought of as a glamorous business, and some designers take it overboard. If a female designer shows up at a client's home wearing a hat, gloves, and seamed stockings (it's been done), the client will immediately have serious reservations. The key to dressing in this business is to dress professionally. You want your clients to take you seriously, as they would any other business owner. You want to project not only your creative side, but your business personality as well.

You don't have to wear boring clothes to dress professionally. If you are a woman, you can pair a hot new color with a simple black skirt and look professional. By adding a designer color, you can show off your color sense. If you prefer to wear a suit, add an unusual pin or scarf. If you are a man, you will have to determine whether you want to wear suits or nice slacks and a shirt. Jeans are too casual for an appointment. The type of appointment you go on should play a role in your decision. If you are concentrating on commercial business, a suit will most likely be appropriate. You can personalize it by adding a colorful tie or vest. If you are wearing slacks, wear a shirt that adds personality to your outfit. I once knew a designer who always wore a pair of unusual socks with his slacks. He claimed it was an instant rapport builder.

Defining Your Business

You need to determine how you will set up your business legally. Your choices are sole proprietorship, partnership, or corporation. There are pluses and minuses to all three types of businesses. I will touch on the basics, but if you are in doubt about which type of business would benefit you the most, contact a lawyer and discuss your options.

Sole Proprietorship

In this type of business, you are it, numero uno. There is no one to challenge your decisions or tell you how to spend the company's money. All the profits made are yours; there is no one to share them with. On the other hand, there is no one to confer with when problems arise, no one to deal with the irate customer when you have a headache, and your opinion is it when trying to decide on the right advertising campaign. You are personally liable as a sole proprietor for all business loans and accounts that you sign for. If you break your leg skiing, a family member has an operation, or something else prevents you from completing your work on time, there will be no one else to take care of your company while you're out of commission. (See the insurance section later in this chapter for possible solutions to this problem, such as bonds and disability insurance.)

Partnership

This type of business can be tricky. Many people go into business with a friend, acquaintance, or family member and experience a huge success. On the other hand, many friendships have been severed and family relationships soured because the partnership went bad. If you are thinking of going into business with someone, make sure you are compatible in every way. When starting this type of business, a partnership agreement is mandatory. This agreement is prepared by an attorney, and it can be costly. It will outline every aspect of your business and answer tricky questions on the chance that they arise. For instance, imagine that you went into business with your best friend. You are the outgoing designer who prefers to work with residential clients, while your partner is a business-minded designer who thrives in the corporate atmosphere. It sounds like the perfect match, so you skip the partnership agreement. After all, if you can't trust your best friend, whom can you trust? Everything goes fine for the first four years, the business is turning a profit, and both of you are living quite comfortably. You are acquiring a large share of the marketplace and your competitors are getting nervous. One of them makes you an offer to buy your business at a substantial profit. You want to jump at the chance—it would mean a lot of up-front cash in your pocket—but your business-minded partner sees the potential of the business and is willing to spend the next five or ten years building it up before even considering a sale. The two of you are at a standstill, both firmly believing that they are right. The partnership is in jeopardy and there is no legal backup. If you had a partnership agreement, there would not be a problem. The partnership agreement would have answered that question before it arose, everything would have been worked out beforehand, and there would be no surprises. Another way to safeguard your business is to invest in partnership insurance—this will cover you against any lawsuits arising from your partner's actions.

Try to find a partner who has the skills that you lack. If you are great in marketing for new customers but lack management skills, be sure your partner is management material. One benefit to having a partner is that she or he will be contributing to the finances of the company. Of course, the partner will also be drawing from the profits. Another advantage is that you will not be entirely responsible for everything. If you get that headache, there will be someone to deal with the irate customer. The key to the success of the partnership is finding the right partner—not an easy task.

Corporation

For the interior design business, I highly recommend that you set it up as a corporation. Unlike most small businesses, your liabilities can be substantial. If you are doing any kind of business, your ongoing accounts can easily total $30,000 at any given time. In a corporation, unlike a sole proprietorship, the corporation is responsible for any debts incurred, not you personally.

Your tax structure will be different if you decide to incorporate. You will probably need to hire a certified public accountant (CPA) to explain the ins and outs of the corporate tax laws. The initial fees are higher in this type of business, but I believe they will pay off in the long run.

Existing Businesses and Franchises

You have the option of buying a design firm that has been in business for a while or buying a franchise, which is the name and operation procedures of a known existing company. Let's discuss each of these.

Existing Companies

In any newspaper in any town you can find interior design businesses for sale. Wouldn't it be easier for me to buy one that is already up and running, you ask? Probably not. This business is commonly referred to as a "blue sky" business, meaning that there are no assets, equipment, or tools that have any real-world value. The biggest asset in this type of company is you, the designer, and the relationship you have built with the community. Customer satisfaction is the key to a successful interior design business. Knowing that, I would find it hard to recommend buying an existing business because there is no way of knowing its true reputation in the marketplace. Another reason is the money: It is relatively inexpensive to open this type of business. When buying an existing business, all you are paying for is the name, and you don't know how good that is.

Franchises

There are a few design franchises on the market, but I highly recommend that you do not consider buying them. The start-up costs are high, and after you have paid the initial fee, you will have to continue to pay the franchiser a portion of your retail sales for the life of your business. You will not (usually) be allowed to choose your own vendors in a franchise; the franchiser will choose them for you. If you have any knowledge at all about this business (and you will after reading this book), you can start your own business for much less money, and you will truly be your own boss.

Your Business Name

Now that your office space is set up and you have decided on the legalities, it's time to name your business. The name you choose for your business is important because it portrays an image to the public, and you want to be sure it's the right one. You will also have to live with the name for as long as you own your business, so make sure you are comfortable with it. There are many considerations when choosing a name for your business. The most often thought of is yellow pages placement. Those companies whose names start with an A will be listed first in the yellow pages of the phone book. Although that is an important consideration, there are other things to think about. The image that your business name portrays is just as important. If you call yourself Cost Plus Window Coverings and Design, you will reach a wide market of new homeowners and people wanting to remodel their homes. They will probably be in the market for window coverings as well as other products. They will also probably be looking for a decent price. Let's say you decide to name your business New Wave Design. Some people may understand that you are an interior design shop, but others may think you are a hair studio. Let's change that and call the business New Wave Interiors. Now that the name is clear, what kind of message does it send? I would think most people who call you would be interested in hiring a designer with a contemporary style of design. I also think it might be hard to reach customers with product-only needs. With a design-only name, you lose out on the bulk of the product business out there. This concept could be argued a thousand different ways, but I firmly hold to my opinion that your company name should reflect a product orientation. In subsequent chapters, we'll use Cost Plus Window Coverings and Design in examples of forms and procedures.

The Paper Trail

The state and federal governments require a great deal of paperwork from small business owners. If you follow the rules and are on time with your tax payments, this should not be a problem. It's just one of those things that you won't want to or won't have time to do, but you must.

Assumed Name or Fictitious Name Certificate

This is a form that you will fill out at your local county courthouse, declaring your intention to go into business. This form registers the name you have chosen for your business. The clerk will scan all the current business names on file, and if your prospective name isn't in conflict with any other business's name, a notary public will validate the document. If another business has already registered the name, you will have to choose another.

Request a certified copy of this document because you will need it to set up your business bank account.

Tax Resale Number

You have to charge taxes on any goods that you sell to your customers. You are, in essence, an agent for the state. It's your job, as an agent of the state, to collect the tax owed and pass it along to the state in the form of quarterly payments. Simply go to your local tax collector's office and apply for a number. The tax rate varies in all states, and your local representative will explain the one that applies to you. Be very careful to pay everything that is due, and pay it on time. I suggest setting up a separate bank account just for the sales tax you collect; this is one way to insure that funds do not accidentally become crossed or that you're not short for the amount due.

Federal ID Number

You will need this if you hire full-time employees in your business. Most of your employees will be contract labor (more about this in chapter 10), so you will not need a Federal ID number. In the off chance that you need to hire a regular employee, contact your local officials to request a number.

Contractor Licenses

Some states require licenses for contractors doing specific jobs. For instance, in California you must have a license to install any type of flooring. Some states, however, such as Texas, do not require any type of contractor licenses. Check with your local authorities to determine what you need a license for and what requirements need to be met.

Business Bank Account

You will need a separate bank account for your business. Most manufacturers will not set up a wholesale account with you unless there is a bank account designated for your business. You will need to show the bank a copy of your assumed name certificate and provide them with your resale number in order to open a business account.

Insurance

According to the Independent Insurance Agents of America, more than one-half of home-based businesses aren't sufficiently insured. The biggest mistake business owners make is believing that they are covered under their homeowners policy, but in reality a typical homeowners policy will only insure business items for $2,500 in your home and will not cover items that are taken out of the home (i.e., when you are on appointments).

Since each business situation is different, you'll need to do some research and determine exactly what your needs are. Use the checklist I've provided to start you thinking about your specific needs.

After you've thought about your specific needs, talk to your insurance agent and determine which of the following policies are right for you and your business.

Insurance Question Checklist

✓ Total amount of business equipment. (Samples, computer, etc.)

✓ Will you carry inventory? If so, how much? (Reduced priced fabric or carpet rolls?)

✓ What will it cost to run your business every month? (Disability)

✓ Will you be working with builders? (Bonds)

✓ What if you broke an antique vase in your customer's home while measuring a window? (Professional liability)

Property insurance. This policy will cover your business equipment, furnishings, and samples.

Business property insurance. This covers business equipment taken out of the home, like credit card machines, laptop computers, and installation tools.

Health insurance. This can be daunting to obtain individually, but check with the organizations listed in the appendix of this book. Most offer group rates and discounts.

Professional liability insurance. If your installer tracked mud on a priceless carpet, this policy would pay the damages.

Business interruption insurance. This policy protects against natural disasters, such as a fire or flood that would keep you from operating your business.

Life insurance. This is especially important if you are the head of household. (Your family depends on you to provide for them.)

Workers compensation and workers compensation insurance. The laws vary in each state, so when you hire employees, check with the authorities to find out what they require.

Auto insurance. Check with your insurance agent to find out what provisions you must add to be insured in the event of an accident while working.

Remember to do your research before you choose an agent. Talk to a few companies, and it wouldn't hurt to get in contact with these organizations:

National Insurance Consumer's Helpline: (800) 942–4242
Independent Insurance Agents of America: (800) 261–4422
Insurance Information Institute: (212) 669–9200

Bonds

Most of your professional workers will be bonded. A carpet layer or other full-time contractor is required in most states to post bond. This means that if you hire a carpet layer and the person messes up the installation, you (and your client) will be protected by the bond. In some cases when working with builders or on commercial jobs, the contract will require that your company be bonded. This gives them the same protection if you somehow mess up the job or are unable to complete it. It is possible in some instances to ask the builder or commercial contact to temporarily add you to their policy. If they won't, check with your insurance agent because the price and guidelines of each policy will depend on the job.

General Liability Insurance

If you are measuring the windows in a client's home and accidentally break a 2,000-year-old vase, who pays for it? Your insurance company, if you carry liability insurance. It's wise to carry liability insurance on your business for many reasons. In addition to the scenario I have just listed, a client could sue you if he or she simply trips on a phone cord in your office and gets hurt. Again, your liability insurance should cover any injuries or damages sustained. Your insurance agent will outline the costs, deductibles, and rules of this particular type of policy.

Disability Insurance

This insurance is especially important if you are running a sole proprietorship, and it is one of the most overlooked policies. With this policy, if you are forced to be out of work because of an accident or something else out of your control, a portion of your salary will be paid by the insurance company for a predetermined period of time. There are many variations to this type of policy, and I suggest that you research your alternatives in depth before making any decisions.

Summary

I have asked you to do a lot of research. You need these cost estimates because now we are going to determine your start-up costs. If you have not already made those phone calls, do it now.

Chapter Three
Start-Up Costs

The next step in setting up your business is to determine what your start-up costs will be. When first starting out in business, you should keep your costs to a minimum, investing only in the necessities. Later, when your business is making a profit, you can add the luxuries if you so desire. In this chapter we will explore the various purchases you will need to make and complete a personalized start-up cost worksheet using the information from your research. The worksheet will give you an idea of how much it will cost to open the doors of your new business. This chapter can be complex, but it is vital to the success of your business, so don't skip over it.

What It Will Cost to Start Your Business

The start-up costs that you need to consider are basic office supplies, a computer and necessary software, samples, advertising, licenses, insurance, telephone, working capital, personal reserve, and any remodeling you may do in setting up your office space. It is impossible for me to provide you with the exact figures of these items because each case will be different. Just make a few phone calls to determine what the charges are in your area for each of the items listed. Then plug those figures into the worksheet I have provided and you will get a reliable picture of the amount of money needed to start your business. This figure will be the basis of your business plan that is discussed in the next chapter. If you have some cash put away and do not plan on applying for a loan, it is still essential that you have a good business plan. Without one, you won't have a good idea where your business is headed, or even if it is going in the right direction. A business trying to make it without a business plan is like a train trying to run without tracks.

Doing the Books

The most common problem with doing financial projections for an interior design business is that most designers aren't that good with numbers. In order to run a successful business of this type, you must be good at design *and* have a business mind. If you have any doubts, hire someone to do your books for you. It will be an additional expense, and one that you probably don't need when you're just starting out, but it may save your business in the long run. It is a rare person who is both creative and analytical. I did my own books for the first four years, and I did fine, but it was a constant struggle. I finally hired a bookkeeper and my life got much easier, but by that time the monthly payment wasn't a burden. It's up to you, but if you find yourself wanting to skip over this section or are having a hard time with it, you may want to consider adding a bookkeeping fee to your start-up cost worksheet. (I have included a blank for it on the sheet just in case.) Call around to determine the costs in your area. Most bookkeeping services start at around $100 and then increase depending on the complexity and volume of your business. If you plan on doing your own bookkeeping, there are good software programs on the market that will make it easier. Do your research to determine which is best suited to your needs. The most popular programs right now are Quickbooks and Peachtree Complete Accounting.

Your research will guide you in filling out the start-up cost worksheet that follows, except for a few areas. Your initial advertising will vary de-

Start-Up Cost Worksheet	
Fixtures and equipment (samples, camera, car, etc.)	$_____
Remodeling costs for new office	$_____
Office supplies	$_____
Business cards and stationery	$_____
Licenses and permits	$_____
Legal and bookkeeping fees	$_____
Insurance	$_____
Telephone deposits and setup fees	$_____
Initial advertising	$_____
Working capital (3 months)	$_____
Personal expenses (3 months)	$_____
TOTAL	$_____

pending on where you live and how much you plan on advertising. I suggest that you read chapter 6 before filling in that blank.

You also will need to plan on having three months of working capital and personal capital in the bank before you start your business. You already know how much it costs you to live (add your mortgage or rent, car payments, food purchases, electric and phone bills, any loan or credit card payments, and miscellaneous expenses). Use the general overhead section of the profit-and-loss worksheet in chapter 4 as a guide to arrive at this number.

Buying and Using a Computer

Fortunately, you're opening a business at a time when computers are easily affordable. But before you jump right in and purchase one, there are a couple of things to consider.

Type: In today's market you can purchase a laptop for only slightly more than a desktop. You'll have to determine what machine will best suit your needs. If you plan to use a scanner for your price lists and formulas, and carry your computer with you, you're obviously better off toting a laptop. On the other hand, if you plan to use a computer mainly to do bookkeeping and business correspondence, you'll probably want a desktop.

Space: If you're limited, the convenience of being able to put away the computer at the end of the workday may be worth the little extra money.

Internet Uses

It's hard, if not impossible, in this business to generate leads with the Internet since most of what you do will be custom, but I have found it helpful in some areas.

Organizations. You can join Interior Design and small business organizations and participate in forums and discussions in order to stay current on the issues and trends. Also, by playing an active role, you may be able to make contacts that could lead to business. I've listed a few organizations in the appendix of this book.

E-mail. This form of communication is quickly replacing "snail mail," and even the telephone, for many people. It's a great time-saving way to keep in contact with your customers, and many manufacturers accept orders via the Internet.

Designing a Web Page

Is it necessary for an interior designer to have a Web presence? It depends on what you expect from it. Basically, there are two types of Web pages: a business card site and a Cyberstore (a site that sells a product). The one you choose, or whether you choose any at all, will depend on your expectations from the Web.

BUSINESS CARD SITE

If you want to merely establish a presence on the Web and not necessarily sell any product, then this is the site for you. On it you would announce to the (Web) world that you are in business and then give a general outline of the services and products that you offer. This approach comes in handy when advertising in the traditional sense, because customers can then use your Web address to get more detailed information about you and your products.

Don't expect to increase sales drastically with this type of site, however. The biggest benefit to setting up a Web site like this is the image that you'll portray to the general public. Establishing a Web presence today is almost mandatory, and those companies that do so will ultimately look more professional than their non-Internet competitors.

Having said that, it's important to understand that you don't need a site like this when just starting out. Your start-up costs should be kept to a minimum in the beginning, and only when you are turning a profit should you consider a Web site (unless you plan to develop a site that actually sells product).

CYBERSTORE

If you are planning for Internet sales to make up a portion of your yearly sales, then you'll need a Web site that allows consumers to purchase those products on-line. In order to accomplish this process, your site will have to contain a catalog of your products, a shopping cart, and the ability to accept credit cards. There are many viable companies that sell home-decor products on-line but few that specialize in more than one. For instance, there are window covering on-line stores, carpet on-line stores, and furniture and fabric on-line stores, but none that successfully sell all interior design products. So if you plan to create an on-line store, it would be wise to select one product to concentrate on. (I would suggest doing some serious on-line research in order to determine the competition and pricing structures in each category before deciding on a product.)

THE BASICS

It is possible to construct a Web site yourself by using one of the various software packages available on today's market. But if you're not technologically minded, you might have to hire a professional to do it for you. Plan to spend a few hundred dollars for the software if you're going to build the site yourself or a few thousand if you plan to hire someone to do it for you.

Next you'll have to determine which server will provide you Internet access and calculate those costs into your start-up budget. Plan to pay an Internet Service Provider approximately $200 per year for hosting services. Try to find a host that offers free e-mail, so that your e-mail address will match your Web site address (and be more memorable).

There are also different packages available—such as Microsoft bcentral ($300 to $500 per year) and Homestead (approximately $160 per year)—that offer complete Web site building software, e-mail, and hosting services.

Finally, you'll have to advertise your Web site, just as you will your off-line business. Look for hints about Internet advertising in chapter 6.

Samples

Samples are the lifeblood of your business. Without them you could not sell your product and services. Each manufacturer produces books of samples that represent its various products in a designer fashion. You will use these samples to show color and help with the expression of your ideas.

You should be able to fill in all of the blanks on the start-up cost worksheet except for the one titled "Fixtures and equipment." Included in this item are samples, and I will discuss them now. There is a sample book for every product that you sell. If you don't know what they look like, visit a home improvement store or a designer showroom and look around. You will be surrounded by carpet binders, fabric books, paint wheels, and window covering sample books. (Every window covering product has its own sample book.) Because you will be working out of your home, you will not be able to rely on the large vignettes and product displays that the larger stores do. (You won't have their high overhead, either!) Instead, you will carry with you the samples of all the products that you sell. There are quite a few manufacturers or vendors for each product. Refer to chapter 9 for a list of them when you get ready to set up your accounts. Each manufacturer will be represented by a salesperson called a manufacturer's representative. It's that person's job to convince you that her or his manufacturer's line is better than the other guy's. As a business owner, you will have to decide what companies you want to work with and what product best suits your and your client's needs. There are some products that are represented by several different manufacturers, and pricing and service will be your deciding factor for whom to do business with.

Sample Books

The prices of sample books vary. Take for instance the window covering samples. The books can run about $250 from some manufacturers, but another one may decide to give them to you for free. Most of the time it is left up to the sales representative to determine the distribution of the company's books. If you can convince sales representatives that you will sell a great amount of their product, they will be more likely to give you the books for free. Of course, that may be hard to do when just starting out in business. This is another argument in favor of working for someone else first. Not only will you get the experience you need, you will also get to know the sales representatives and increase your chances of not having to pay for their samples. If you still want to jump right in and you can't persuade any of the sales representatives to give you the books for free, keep trying. As your sales increase with them, they will be more likely to give you one for free every now and then. Smaller manufacturers are usually more liberal with their samples.

Some manufacturers offer a sample rebate program. This program works just like coupons; it can be like receiving free samples if you use it correctly. When you buy a $250 sample book from one of these manufacturers, you will also receive five $50 coupons. Every time you sell that product, you use one of the coupons when it's time to pay the invoice. All you have to do is sell the product five times and the book will be paid for. This is not only a good way to save money on sample books, it's also very motivational!

One obstacle you may run into when purchasing samples is the "sample plan." Some manufacturers insist that if you do business with them, you must purchase sight unseen, preselected samples from them every month or so. Wallpaper and the larger fabric companies are notorious for this practice. The idea behind the plan is that you own a showroom and have plenty of room to stock their samples. These sample plans vary in cost, but I have seen them run anywhere from $200 to $1,500 per month. Obviously, it is not prudent for a home-based designer to work with these programs, but don't worry—there are other options. The most obvious is to not do business with these manufacturers. There are an abundant number of suppliers out there who are willing to sell to you on less stringent terms. The problem is that most of the companies that use sample plans are well known in the consumer marketplace. Because of this, some of your customers may request that you use a particular brand on their job. You don't want to have to outlay that kind of money on the off chance that one of your customers will request one of these products. On the other hand, you want to be able to accommodate their needs. Enter designer showrooms.

Designer Showrooms

A designer showroom is a privately owned business that sells products to designers at discounted prices. The showroom will generally carry a large selection of drapery fabrics, upholstery fabrics, wallpaper, carpet, wood and vinyl flooring, ceramic tile, hard window coverings (miniblinds, verticals, shutters, etc.), and paint. Some of the more sophisticated showrooms will also carry or have access to lighting, furniture, and accessories. Great, you say, why even bother to purchase my own samples? The answer is money. Although these showrooms are a terrific resource for a designer in a pinch, there is a price to pay. These showrooms are in business to make money, and that money comes out of your profit. Rather than selling you the product at a wholesale rate, they add a markup to everything that they sell. That means if you are doing a carpet job and would normally buy a piece of carpet for $2,000 from a manufacturer, you might have to pay up to $2,600 for it at one of these showrooms. Since most of your bidding will be done on a competitive basis, the $600 will come out of your pocket, not your client's. That means if you were planning on selling the job for $4,000 and making a $2,000 profit, you are now down to a $1,400 profit. The use of designer showrooms sparingly can be a helpful tool to today's designer, but be smart and use them only when it's necessary.

I have included a sample comparative chart to help you determine which manufacturer is giving you the best deal on samples. Gather all the information on each company you are considering and stack it in piles according to the product. For example, put all the

Comparative Chart for Samples

TYPE OF PRODUCT	MANUFACTURER	SAMPLE COST	REBATES	FINAL COSTS

window covering manufacturers in one pile, the carpet companies in another, and so on. Then fill out a chart for each type of product and determine which one will give you the best deal. That is the manufacturer you should buy from.

Pricing Your Products

In this type of business you are somewhat in the middle. You are not making the goods yourself—you are buying them from a manufacturer and then reselling them. In this chapter we will discuss the process of arriving at your selling price. To do this, you first need to understand how to determine your purchase price from the manufacturer. (These numbers are considered part of your costs of doing business, so they won't show up on any of the worksheets.)

Another area of negotiation is discounts. A discount is the factor that determines how much you will pay for a product. This business is not like most businesses; you will not get a wholesale price list and figure your selling price from that. To make things even more confusing, all of the different types of manufacturers price their products differently. I will briefly discuss each of the types of products and how they are priced so that you will be prepared when you set up your accounts.

Window Coverings

In the hard window covering industry, there is no such thing as a wholesale price list. A designer is given discounts off the retail price list to arrive at the buying price.

Every designer will be given the same retail price list; it's the discount that determines how much you will pay for the product. For instance, if you have a client who wants to buy one miniblind, you would look at the retail price list and determine what percentage off to give the client. In some parts of the country, 70 percent off retail price would be normal in this instance. If the retail price of the blind was $100, that would make your selling price $30 ($100 – 70% = $30). Now let's imagine that your sales representative has given you a discount of 50/50. That means your cost on the blind is $25 ($100 – 50% = $50 – 50% = $25) In an area where a 70 percent off discount is competitive, clearly a 50/50 discount would not give you enough of a profit.

This is where your negotiation skills come in. Most manufacturers have a standard discount sheet that they hand out to anyone who will take it. People who have been in business for a while realize that those discounts are negotiable. Now, so do you. The hard window coverings are perhaps the most negotiable. I've seen miniblind discounts of 50/50/20/10/5. Sounds ridiculous, but most manufacturers consider miniblinds a lost leader item—that is, an item advertised so cheap that its only purpose is to draw people in. By selling miniblinds at such a discount, you then have a chance to sell your client a better and more expensive product as well. There is an in-depth discussion about this technique, called up-selling, in chapter 7.

Hard window covering manufacturers also give discounts on their products such as vertical blinds, pleated and cellular shades, silhouettes, vignettes, shutters, roller shades, and wood blinds. The discounts vary from designer to designer, so it will be up to you to negotiate the best discount that you can.

Carpet

Carpet companies are a different matter altogether. They operate from a wholesale price list versus a retail price list. Those prices are also negotiable. There are many of these price lists, and your job is to be assigned the one that quotes the lowest prices. There will be two prices for each of the carpets listed, one for a piece of carpet and one for a roll. (Each manufacturer has a different idea of what constitutes a roll, so check with your sales representative.) Ask your sales representative for the best price available because this is a highly competitive field. You will probably have to start out by paying more for the carpet until you build a track record of sales. Unless you plan on specializing in carpet, this will probably not be your best-selling item; it's just too hard to compete with the larger carpet stores. There are many of them that will install carpet for less than you will be able to buy it for. Most of your carpet jobs will come from "complete package" jobs, in other words, jobs where you quote the customer a single price for designing an entire room or house.

Manufacturer Discount Comparative Worksheet

Manufacturer

Product		Discount		Product		Discount
Product		Discount		Product		Discount
Product		Discount		Product		Discount
Product		Discount		Product		Discount

Manufacturer

Product		Discount		Product		Discount
Product		Discount		Product		Discount
Product		Discount		Product		Discount
Product		Discount		Product		Discount

Manufacturer

Product		Discount		Product		Discount
Product		Discount		Product		Discount
Product		Discount		Product		Discount
Product		Discount		Product		Discount

Manufacturer

Product		Discount		Product		Discount
Product		Discount		Product		Discount
Product		Discount		Product		Discount
Product		Discount		Product		Discount

Wallpaper

Wallpaper companies also operate in an entirely different manner. It will be hard, if not impossible, to find a wallpaper company that will sell to you without your subscribing to a sample plan. The larger the plan, the bigger your discounts will be. The larger plans are also the most expensive. When you're just starting out in business, it's hard to justify signing up with one of these plans. In the beginning, I suggest that you use a designer showroom or share samples with another designer. Many home-based designers share their resources to combat issues like this. You can meet them through organizations or simply call one who does not do business in your area and suggest a meeting.

I have provided you with a manufacturer discount comparative worksheet that will help you keep the various manufacturers' discounts straight. You will use this worksheet throughout your time in business because your discounts will constantly change. You always need to know from whom you are getting the best price. For instance, if you decide to do business with company A, but company B wants your business, it may offer you larger discounts to entice you to switch your business. Use the worksheet by filling in the pertinent information every time you meet with or talk to a sales representative and your life will be much easier.

Chapter Four

Writing Your Business Plan

Think of a business plan as a road map. You wouldn't drive a car across the country without a road map, would you? You shouldn't start a business without one either. It is possible to run a business without a plan, but you will put yourself at an immediate disadvantage. When starting your own business, it's important to do everything you can to ensure your success, and a good business plan is an excellent start. You're probably thinking that it sounds as if I'm preparing you for something you're not going to want to do. I am. Unless you're the type of person who thrives on numbers and projections (and most interior designers aren't), this will not be the most enjoyable part of your business. But it's absolutely necessary.

Not every business plan reads the same; it depends on what purpose it will serve. If you are going to present it to a bank or another lender for start-up capital, you will need to focus on the hows and whens of repayment. If you don't plan on seeking funds, write the business plan for yourself. What would you like to know? Perhaps you want to project your future income, or maybe you need to know how many jobs you have to do in order to make a specific income. Wouldn't it be handy to know how many years you should wait before hiring an employee? Whatever your purpose, the business plan will set you on the right track toward a successful business. I'm going to guide you step-by-step through this process and make it as easy as possible.

Preparing Your Statement of Purpose

By the time I got around to doing this, I had been in business for five years and employed seven people. I felt as if I didn't know where my business was headed; I needed direction. I spent hundreds of dollars hiring a motivation expert to come in. I spent three hours with this expert and my employees, and we wrote a group statement of purpose. I couldn't help feeling that other people were shaping my company image. Even worse was the fact that I was paying them to do so! All of this is just not necessary. You can take thirty minutes right now and write your own. Here is what I paid $750 for:

> *Our goal is to design our customers' homes with a*
> *sense of style that is unique. We will always keep*
> *humor as a constant in our work attitude. Our*
> *customers' satisfaction is the ultimate goal.*

Your statement of purpose should define what makes your business unique. Sure, you want to design homes, but how? Will you concentrate on one style of design or have an eclectic style? Will you work with wealthy clients or concentrate on middle-income families? Will you put customer satisfaction above everything else? (If you said no to this question, please refer to chapter 1.) You should be able to answer all these questions with your statement of purpose. Make it short and brief, but it should portray the image you want for your business.

Providing Your General Business Description

This is the area of the plan where you should detail the basics of your business. The information in this section should include: your business name, the legal setup of your business (sole proprietorship, partnership, or corporation), the name of the owner or partners, the main source of income (residential or commercial), and the business address.

Summarizing Your Business

Any lender will want to know how you plan to repay the loan and what the financial potential of the business is. In this section of the business plan, you should detail the type of clientele you plan to work with and forecast the potential business.

Acquiring Clientele

Hopefully, you have already decided whether you want to work in the commercial field or the residential market. Now you have to determine how you will attract those potential clients. If you want to work in the residential field, make a list of all the new subdivisions within a 30-mile radius (or however far you are willing to travel for business) and include those in your plan. Include your plans for acquiring this potential business. The same goes for commercial clients. How are you going to persuade them to do business with your company—cold-call their offices, advertise in trade magazines? State it. (Chapter 6 will provide an in-depth discussion of this topic.)

Figuring Your Sales Potential

The interior design business is different from most businesses because you can't place a specific price on the individual products that you sell. You will do any number of combinations of products; you may never do the same job twice. For instance, one client may require new carpet, some upholstery, and seven vertical blinds. That job may total $7,000. Your next job may only entail twenty miniblinds for a new home. That job would probably run about $1,500. (These figures are to be used only as rough examples because prices vary in different parts of the country.) I ran my figures and came up with an average cost of $734 per job, so we'll use that as an example for your forecasts. If you plan on working full time and are ambitious enough to aggressively market Realtors, architects, and new neighborhoods, you could reasonably expect to do at least five jobs per month your first year in business. At $734 per job, your sales potential would be $3,670 per month.

Your next step is to turn your monthly projections into yearly projections. If you were able to keep up the pace of five jobs per month for the entire year, your potential sales would be $44,040. Now let's say the next year you manage to double the jobs that you do to ten per month. Your yearly sales would jump to $88,080. By the third year, you've got more business than you can handle, so you hire someone. Your new employee is able to complete seven jobs per month. Add that to your ten and that brings your sales figure to $149,736 for the year (17 x $734 x 12 = $149,736). Do this month by month and then extend your figures to five years.

When you calculate your figures, be realistic about what you can do, how much time you will have to invest in your business, and any vacation time you plan on taking. Do you live in an area that is depressed, or is the economy on an upswing? What do economists forecast for the next few years? Use these figures to guide you in your projections.

Defining your Business

This is the part of the plan that you will use to sell your business ideas to a potential lender. When writing this section, imagine how you'll be viewed by the person lending the money. What will you offer to the public that will make people want to do business with you? Do you have any experience in the field? Are you an accomplished salesperson? Do you have an uncanny knack for putting colors together? If so, state it. Make a list of the products and services you plan to offer. Your list might look something like the one that follows.

You also will need to include in this section of your plan what your intended charges are for your products and services. Read the section of this book about shopping the competition for a detailed guide on how to set your prices. A lender will feel more confident in you if you've done the market research and are knowledgeable in the field. In addition to that, knowing what market you are trying to penetrate can only increase your chances of success. Provide a list of your estimated charges for each of the products. Since it will be impossible to list each price separately (how many sizes of miniblinds are there, anyway?),

Products Offered	Services Offered
Miniblinds	Installation of blinds
Vertical blinds	Installation of verticals
Shutters	Installation of shutters
Carpet, tile, and vinyl	Installation of all flooring
Draperies	Installation of draperies
Wallpaper	Installation of wallpaper
Miscellaneous parts	Repair of all products
Upholstery fabrics	Upholstery work
	Design consultation

select one size for each product. For example, use a 35-by-60-inch window size for your window covering products. Use a 12-by-12-foot room size for all of your flooring products, and a 12-by-8-foot wall size for wallpaper prices. Be sure to know what discounts are standard in your area and base your prices on that. As for your design consultation fees, shop around and find out what your competition is charging. Most beginning designers charge between $25 and $35 per hour. Be careful of "lowballing" (selling the product or service at a substantially lower price than the market demands). Bankers will be wary of this tactic because these types of businesses don't tend to stay in business for very long.

Devising Your Marketing Strategy

We will go into the different marketing strategies in detail in chapter 6, so read it before you complete this portion of your plan. This part of the plan will outline how you are going to go after your business. Include every marketing strategy you plan to use. (Some of the things we will talk about in chapter 6 are calling on new home Realtors, yellow page advertisement, meetings and associations, asking architects for business, passing out flyers, cold-calling homeowners in the subdivisions, giving product presentations to Realtor groups, and so on.) This section of the plan will let the lender know whether you have a realistic idea of how to attract business. Again, I want to remind you, if you don't plan on seeking funds from a lender, do this plan anyway. Can you see so far how much it will help you in running your business?

Forecasting Your Company Equipment and Setup

This is where the start-up costs worksheet that you have completed comes in handy. In this section you will be forecasting the equipment you will need over the next few years, including office furniture, computer equipment, automobiles, samples, and tools. If, as in the previous example, you plan on hiring another designer in three years, you must take into consideration the fact that you will need to add a complete set of sample books, tools, and possibly even a larger storage space to handle the additional incoming product. Will you provide your new employee with an automobile, insurance, paid holidays? All these considerations must be reflected in your figures.

Determining Your Organizational Setup

You know after reading the basic job description in chapter 1 that you will have many organizational duties. Once your business gets larger, you can think about hiring someone to take some of the load off you, but in the beginning, you're it. For this section give a brief description of what running your company will entail. Tell of plans to add employees as you see fit. You also might include in this section a list of your skills that will benefit the company. See the following example of a projected five-year employee plan.

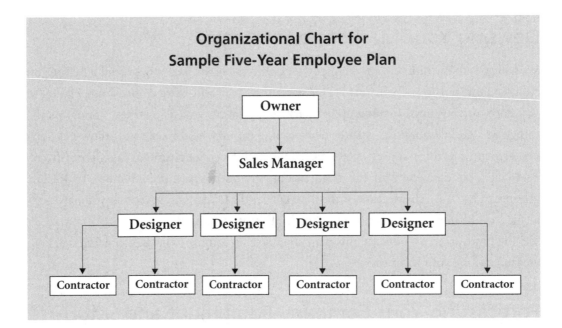

Organizational Chart for Sample Five-Year Employee Plan

Making Financial Projections

As I stated in chapter 3, doing the financial end of the business can be tricky for most interior designers. This section of the business plan will help you determine how much it will cost to start and run your business. If you have decided to do your own books, you will have no problem with it. If you have decided to hire someone to help you with your books, you may want to ask for that person's help on this section.

Creating a Balance Sheet

A balance sheet will help you know, at any given time, what overall financial shape your business is in, but the figures will change weekly. You need to keep constant tabs on the financial status of your business so you can make intelligent decisions on purchases. For example, when planning your advertising campaign for the next month, you first have to know how much money you have to spend on it. Your business account is not like your personal accounts; believe it or not, you may not always know the exact amount of money in it. The balance sheet will give you an overview of your position. It separates your assets (those things in your business that can bring you immediate cash) and your liabilities (any accounts or other obligations that will take cash out of your account). By subtracting your liabilities from your assets, you will be able to determine how much available money you have. When you fill out the assets portion of the worksheet, you will list the money you have in your bank accounts (checking and savings), the amount of petty cash you have as well as any other cash you have on hand, your total accounts receivable (money owed to you), and your furniture and equipment less depreciation. The liability section of this worksheet calls for your accounts payable (money that you owe, such as outstanding invoices for products), the total amount of any loans that you have outstanding, the amount of your lease (if applicable), and the total amount of taxes due. The last section of the worksheet analyzes your equity (the actual amount of money at hand). You will need to fill in your current net profit (profit after expenses). Now subtract your salary from this amount to arrive at your sum total.

Generating a Profit-and-Loss Statement

This report will tell you whether your business is making a profit or, heaven forbid, a loss. It can also serve a few other important purposes. As you have now discovered, you will be buying from many different manufacturers. We discussed how to negotiate discount rates in chapter 3. One of the most important things the manufacturers will consider when assigning you a discount is the dollar amount of sales that you do with them. As your sales increase, so do your discounts. This report will not only help you keep track of the overall health of your business, it also will break down the dollar amount of business that you do

Sample Balance Worksheet

Balance worksheet as of _____ (Date) _____

For _____ (Name of business) _____

ACCOUNT	BALANCE
Assets	
Cash in bank/checking and savings	$_____
Petty cash	$_____
Other cash on hand	$_____
Accounts receivable	$_____
Office furniture and equipment	$_____
less depreciation	– $_____
TOTAL ASSETS	$_____
Liabilities and Equity	
Liabilities	
Accounts payable	$_____
Loans payable	$_____
Leases payable	$_____
Taxes	$_____
TOTAL LIABILITIES	$_____
Equity	
Current capital	$_____
Current net profit	$_____
Less owner's salary	$_____
TOTAL EQUITY	$_____
TOTAL LIABILITIES AND EQUITY	$_____

with each supplier separately. Some companies will do this report once a month, others just once a year. I recommend, especially in the beginning, doing a profit-and-loss statement once a month. If you have a computer program like the ones I cited earlier, all you have to do is press a button and the report will be generated for you. (The program is tied into your bank records, so the information is simply formatted into the report.) An example of a typical profit-and-loss statement for an interior design business follows.

Begin the worksheet by logging in your total amount of sales as well as any other income that relates to your business. Next, you need to determine the amount of money that it costs you to sell the products. You will do this by entering the total amount of invoices you have for that period. You will notice that there are spaces for three different manufacturers after each category. You will use more than one manufacturer for each product, and by filling in the costs separately, you will be able to keep tabs on how much money you are spending with each vendor. Add the total amount of costs and subtract that from your gross sales; that will give you your total gross profit.

Next, you will need to total your overhead expenses for the period of time that the profit-and-loss statement is to cover. Once you have that total, subtract it from your gross profit figure and you will finally arrive at your net profit total.

Making Cash Flow Projections

When operating a business, you will constantly have cash coming in and going out because you will be collecting checks from clients and paying vendors and bills. Your jobs and the sizes of them will also fluctuate. Because of this you will need to keep constant tabs on your cash flow. It is entirely possible for a large job to leave your bank account depleted at the end of the month. Here's an example of how that works. Say you've been going along smoothly the entire month, and then a $20,000 job lands in your lap. You're thrilled! You order the materials, hire the contractors, and set out to do the job. As in all jobs, you have collected a down payment that amounts to one-half of the total job. Within a week, the bills start arriving from the suppliers in addition to the bills from your other jobs. The $10,000 deposit from your client is not enough to cover your costs of the job. You are in a bind; you have invoices that you can't cover because you won't get the final payment from your client until the job is completed. You have a huge order sitting on your books, but you are

Sample Profit-and-Loss Worksheet

PROFIT-AND-LOSS WORKSHEET FOR _Date_ **THROUGH** _Date_

INCOME

Gross sales $_____

Other income $_____

TOTAL INCOME $_____

COST OF SALES EXPENSES

Blinds

Manufacturer # 1 $_____

Manufacturer # 2 $_____

Manufacturer # 3 $_____

TOTAL BLINDS $_____

Fabric

Manufacturer # 1 $_____

Manufacturer # 2 $_____

Manufacturer # 3 $_____

TOTAL FABRIC $_____

Flooring

Manufacturer # 1 $_____

Manufacturer # 2 $_____

Manufacturer # 3 $_____

TOTAL FLOORING $_____

Labor

Manufacturer # 1 $_____

Manufacturer # 2 $_____

Manufacturer # 3 $_____

TOTAL LABOR $_____

Wallpaper

Manufacturer # 1 $\hspace{4cm}$ \$_____

Manufacturer # 2 $\hspace{4cm}$ \$_____

Manufacturer # 3 $\hspace{4cm}$ \$_____

TOTAL WALLPAPER $\hspace{1cm}$ \$_____

TOTAL COST OF SALES EXPENSES $\hspace{1cm}$ \$_____

GROSS PROFIT $\hspace{1cm}$ \$_____
(sales minus cost of sales expenses)

General overhead expenses

Accounts payable $\hspace{3cm}$ \$_____

Advertising $\hspace{3cm}$ \$_____

Automobile $\hspace{3cm}$ \$_____

Cell phone $\hspace{3cm}$ \$_____

Education $\hspace{3cm}$ \$_____

Electric bill $\hspace{3cm}$ \$_____

Freight $\hspace{3cm}$ \$_____

Insurance $\hspace{3cm}$ \$_____

Legal and professional fees $\hspace{1cm}$ \$_____

Miscellaneous fees $\hspace{2cm}$ \$_____

Office supplies $\hspace{3cm}$ \$_____

Phone rental $\hspace{3cm}$ \$_____

Referral fees $\hspace{3cm}$ \$_____

Rent paid $\hspace{3cm}$ \$_____

Samples $\hspace{3cm}$ \$_____

Taxes $\hspace{3cm}$ \$_____

Telephone $\hspace{3cm}$ \$_____

Wages $\hspace{3cm}$ \$_____

TOTAL GENERAL OVERHEAD EXPENSES $\hspace{1cm}$ \$_____

NET PROFIT $\hspace{1cm}$ \$_____
(gross profit minus total general overhead expenses)

presently operating in the red. This is called *cash poor*, and it will happen to you if you don't consistently do your cash flow projections.

Use the following cash flow projections worksheet in your business consistently and it will help curtail hardship.

Cash Flow Projections Worksheet								
Month	**Cash in Bank**	**Petty Cash**	**Sales**	**Collections**	**Total Cash**	**Expenses**	**Projected Expenses**	**Cash Balance**
Jan.								
Feb.								
Mar.								
Apr.								
May								
June								
July								
Aug.								
Sept.								
Oct.								
Nov.								
Dec.								

I recommend preparing this form once a month. Simply log in all cash you have on hand as well as any cash you expect to receive by the end of the month (such as any accounts receivable due) and then total these numbers. Then deduct your fixed expenses along with any projected expenses and you will arrive at your expected cash balance for the month. This will prepare you for situations like the one I mentioned in the example. If, at the end of the month, you have an expected cash balance of $2,000 and you receive that $20,000 job, here are a few things you can do to alleviate the problem.

Acquiring a Short-Term Loan

If you have a good relationship with your banker, you may be able to persuade her or him to give you a short-term loan. Take in your invoice showing that you have the business and explain that it will cost more than the deposit to process the order. As long as you have kept up with any loan payments you have, the bank should have no problem giving you a short-term loan. The purpose of this loan is to provide you with the needed cash in order to finish the job. The loan will be payable when the job is complete.

Negotiating with Your Vendors

Every manufacturer that you will deal with will have a credit department and a credit manager. If you find yourself in a situation where you need more time to pay an invoice, call the credit manager and try to negotiate more time. For instance, if you are on a thirty-day pay period with your manufacturer, ask for an extension of sixty days for the large job. As long as your credit is current, the manufacturer should be open to discussion.

Asking for a Larger Deposit

Another avenue for dealing with this cash flow problem is to ask for a larger deposit from your customer. If you explain that you need to collect more money up front to help cover the costs, the customer may be willing to work with you. But you have to be careful not to present an image of a business that can't handle large jobs. I recommend using this tactic only as a last resort. Instead, strive to maintain a good working relationship with your banker and manufacturers so that if the need arises, you will have the first two options.

Sources for Start-Up Capital

While we're on the subject of financing, let's explore your options for financing your business. Following are ideas, ranging from the traditional to more alternative approaches.

- *Family and friends.* It's estimated that 85 percent of all new capital is borrowed from family and friends. This is the friendliest, easiest way to secure capital for your new business. I strongly suggest tapping these resources before going to a bank or another lender. After all, if you were going through a dry spell in your business, would your family really call the note due?
- *Banks.* This is the most often thought of way to finance a new business, but in reality less than 15 percent of new businesses go to a bank for a loan. If you decide that it's best for you, be prepared with a strong business plan and proposal, and be ready to answer numerous questions regarding your business.
- *Venture capitalists.* Increasingly, venture capitalists are looking toward strong home-based businesses to invest in, but most are interested in businesses that are on the verge of tremendous growth. This may be a great source of financing when you need capital to expand your business.
- *Credit cards.* Use this as a last resort for start-up costs because of high interest rates, but know that you have the option of getting a cash advance on your card if need be.
- *Defer payments.* Another last-resort tactic is to defer your mortgage and car payment. Speak to your loan officer, and request that your payments be deferred for one or two months. During this time you'll be responsible for the interest only, and that will give you a good sum of money for your start-up costs.

Chapter Five

Record Keeping

A s I have mentioned previously, the interior design business is one of details. You have to be able to design with a sense of style as well as keep track of the books. If you doubt yourself as to your financial abilities, don't hesitate to hire someone to help you. There are two types of people who can deal with that part of your business: a bookkeeper and an accountant. I will start this chapter by explaining the differences between the two.

Bookkeepers

A bookkeeper is someone who keeps track of your daily transactions (accounts receivable and accounts payable). For a small business the bookkeeper will generally come in once a week and enter all of the money that you've collected into the accounts receivable column and write checks for any outstanding invoices you may have. Then the person will log those checks into your accounts payable column. If you don't feel comfortable having someone with signature access to your accounts, you can pay your own invoices and the bookkeeper will then enter the data. This part of the bookkeeping is not hard; it just needs to be done in a consistent manner. It's easy to get behind and lose track of the status of your business and what direction it's headed. A good computer software program will make the work faster and easier, but if you can't afford a computer system, a manual system will work just as well.

Accountants

An accountant would probably be the best value for your money. If you keep track of your daily transactions and then take that information to an accountant, he or she will use it to create reports, such as the profit-and-loss statement that we discussed in chapter 4. You should think of an accountant as your financial partner, someone able to give advice on various financial aspects of your business. For instance, if you have a good relationship with your accountant and you are considering expanding your business, he or she would be the best person to talk with about it. Your accountant has the ability to stand back and take a look at things from a purely financial aspect.

Your tax form will look a little different now that you own a business, and an accountant will be able to help you with that, too. The accountant will complete the forms due at the end of the year as well as show you how to set up your business in order to reduce your tax debt. It is entirely possible to do your own books and run your own reports, but I highly recommend hiring an accountant to do your tax returns and to keep an eye on the overall health of your business (especially if you decide to incorporate).

Keeping Track of Your Money

You will need a system to keep track of the dollars coming in and going out. I've found that a single-entry bookkeeping system is the easiest way to do that for this type of business. On a daily basis simply enter any money you have collected from clients and then record any debits that you have made to your account. Then subtract the debits from the credits, and you should have a balance. Doing this calculation weekly will help you keep tabs on the status of your business. An example of what your weekly ledger might look like follows on the next page.

Some businesses will use an accrual accounting method for their records. When you use this method, money that is owed to you is recorded as collected money. I don't recommend that system for this type of business because of the way your money will be collected. When you accept a job, you will always ask for a deposit that totals one-half of the total amount of the job. Some jobs may only take one week to complete; in that case, you would collect the balance in a week. Other jobs can take two months or more to complete, and you would not be paid the balance until then. Jobs that consist of more than one type of

Sample Weekly Accounting Ledger

Accounting Records For The Week Of _____ Date _____

For _____ Name of business _____

Income
_____

Date _____ SM _____ Amount $ _____

Date _____ SM _____ Amount $ _____

Date _____ SM _____ Amount $ _____

Date _____ SM _____ Amount $ _____

Date _____ SM _____ Amount $ _____

TOTAL INCOME $_____

Expenses
_____

Rent $ _____

Electricity $ _____

Phone $ _____

Debt payments $ _____

Salary $ _____

Commissions $ _____

Advertising payments $ _____

Manufacturer payments $ _____

Contract labor payments $ _____

Freight $ _____

TOTAL PAYMENTS $ _____

CURRENT BALANCE $ _____

product are even more complicated. If you sell a job that includes miniblinds, carpet, and draperies, you will collect the deposit of one-half of the total job. The miniblinds will come in first, so you will collect the balance for them approximately one week later. The carpet will probably be ready to be installed one week after the blinds, so you will collect the carpet balance then. Finally, the draperies should be in two to three weeks after that, and you'll finally collect the remaining balance. Can you see why you wouldn't want to use the accrual method? You would have recorded the total balance for the job five to six weeks earlier than you had the money in the bank. The cash method records deposits only when there is money ready to be put in the bank. The single-entry method of bookkeeping will give you a more realistic picture of your business.

Typical Progress-of-Sales Invoice	
Total Sale	$ 4,200.00
Less 50% deposit	– $ 2,100.00
Balance Due	$ 2,100.00
Miniblind balance pd.	– $ 350.00
Balance forward	$ 1,750.00
Carpet balance pd.	– $ 750.00
Balance forward	$ 1,000.00
Drapery balance pd.	– $ 1,000.00
Balance Due	$ - 0 -

Accounts Payable and Receivable Files

You will need to keep track of money that is due in and bills that are to be paid out. This process doesn't have to be complicated. As a matter of fact, it can be handled with three expandable file folders: accounts receivable, delinquent accounts, and accounts payable. I'll discuss each one individually.

Accounts Receivable

Accounts receivable are the moneys that are owed to you. Once in a while you will work with a customer and you won't get paid immediately. You might agree to finance the customer, as we will talk about later in this chapter, or you may be working with a commercial client whose payment methods are different than a residential client. You must have a method to help you keep track of this money. You're probably thinking right now that there's no way you're going to forget anyone who owes you money, but you will. You will have so many jobs going on at one time and so many details to remember that a $100 invoice will slip your mind faster than you might think. File the invoices alphabetically by the last name of your client (commonly referred to as the *sidemark,* or SM). Any invoices in this file reflect money that is owed to you. When the invoice is paid, mark it as such and file it in the appropriate customer file.

Delinquent Accounts

Go through the accounts receivable file once a month and send out any delinquent notices that are necessary. If a customer becomes delinquent with an invoice, start taking steps to collect your money. If after numerous phone calls and letters from you the customer still hasn't paid the bill, one option is to assign the debt to a collection agency. The figures vary, but the agency will take a percentage of the amount owed to you.

Another way to collect the debt is to file a lien against the property that you've worked on. Every state varies in its procedures, but as a general rule you as contractor have the right to place a lien on the property you've worked on within a certain number of days after the work is complete. (The amount of time varies, so check with your local authorities.) If you have to place a lien, it will sit on the records collecting interest until the homeowner sells the house or tries to refinance it. The title company will then search the records for any outstanding liens and pay them off with the proceeds of the sale. This is a drastic measure, but you won't have to pay a collection agency a percentage of your profits. Of course you may have to wait years to collect your money plus interest.

Accounts Payable

Accounts payable are the invoices that are owed by you to your vendors and contractors. It's entirely possible to have ten invoices on the same job, so you'll need a system to keep track of them. The easiest way to do this is to use the same system that you use for your accounts receivable, but with another expandable file folder to file the invoices away after they've been paid. Your credit terms will be different with each of your vendors, so it's wise to look through this file weekly to avoid any late payments. Simply file each invoice under the name of the vendor; for example, Apple Miniblinds would be filed under A, and Zebra Carpets would be filed under Z. After you have paid the invoice, write *paid* and the date and the number of the check you used to pay it and file it in the accounts payable paid file. Any COD (cash on delivery) account invoices should go directly into the paid file. If you are negotiating better discounts with a vendor and want to prove how much business you have given that vendor over the last six months, simply pull invoices from the paid file and total them.

Change Orders

There will be times when you will be rolling through a job and the customer will change her or his mind about which carpet to use, or even about the trim color chosen for the bedspread. That's when a change order comes in. When you first accept a job, you will ask the customer to sign a contract that spells out the details and dollar amount of a job. (More about this contract later in this chapter.) If *anything* changes from the original contract, you should have the customer sign a change order, which is a form that spells out the exact changes as well as any dollar amount that changes. I cannot stress the importance of paying strict attention to the details of the contract and change orders. When a customer is doing a lot of work on his or her home, the details can get fuzzy. If a customer remembers that the draperies were supposed to be blue and they were made pink, you would be in a

Sample Change Order

Change Order

Date _____

Purchase Order Number _____

Customer Name _____

Address _____

Phone Number _____

Item to Be Changed _____

_____

_____

_____

Difference in Price (+ or –) _____

I (the homeowner) agree that the above change items are true and requested by me. I will pay the difference in price if it is higher than the original invoice. I authorize the contractor to complete the changes as stated above.

_____   _____
CONTRACTOR   HOMEOWNER

---

tough position unless you had a contract or a change order with the customer's signature on it showing the selection or change.

There was a time a change order saved me from a major loss. I was working with a married couple and designing draperies for their entire home. The job totaled approximately $15,000. About a quarter of the way through the job, the wife decided she didn't want a drape on the atrium window; she thought it would block the view. I deleted the drapery from the order, subtracted the amount from the total balance due, and had her sign a change order. Four weeks later when the job was complete, we installed the draperies. When everything was hung, I went to my clients and asked for the balance due, about $7,000. The husband refused to pay, claiming that I had left out one of the draperies—the one in the atrium. He told me he wouldn't pay for any of the job until I installed the atrium drapery. Luckily, I had the change order that his wife had signed and pulled it out to show him. He reluctantly conceded and paid me the balance. If I hadn't had a change order, I might have had to provide him with an additional drape (at no charge since I had already subtracted the amount from the invoice) and waited another two to four weeks for my money. I have provided a sample change order form that you can use in your business.

Customer Contracts

It is imperative to have all customers sign a contract before you begin work in their home. A contract serves to protect you and your customer from the inevitable discrepancies that occur when dealing with custom products. Let me give you a typical example of what can happen without a contract. Let's imagine that you take an order from a client to install a room of carpet in her home. The color she's chosen is not in stock and has to be ordered from the mill. You confirm the delivery date with the mill as two weeks from the order date. Your customer signs a contract and you order the carpet. Because your business is new, the carpet mill requires a 50 percent deposit on the order to get it processed. You write the mill a check and sit back and wait. Two days before the order is due, the mill calls you to tell you the carpet has been delayed another two weeks. When the customer hears the news, she is so angry that she tells you to cancel the order. If you were to cancel the order, you would be out the 50 percent deposit that you sent the mill because that money is nonrefundable once the mill has started work on the order. Luckily, your client signed a contract, part of which states that you cannot be held responsible for acts of nature or manufacturing delays.

Here's another example that happens to be true. A few years ago my business was booming and I had quite a few orders pending. Then a flood hit the Midwest. Everything coming from that region of the country was stranded and I couldn't fill the orders. If I hadn't had my clients sign contracts, they might have been tempted to cancel their orders, and

I would have been out of a lot of money that month. I hope these examples have sold you on the importance of having your clients sign contracts.

Credit Accounts for Your Business

Taking care of your personal and business credit is one of the most important things you can do for the growth of your business. If your personal credit rating isn't spotless, it will inhibit your business growth. One way you can help keep your credit in line is to stay on top of your record keeping. You will be overwhelmed with a daily barrage of paperwork. Be sure you know when your bills are due, and pay them on time. I will discuss various methods in this chapter that will help you with the organization of your paperwork to keep your credit report clear of blemishes. When you buy from the various manufacturers, they will offer you terms, or an open account, if your credit record is clear. If it isn't, they will probably set you up on a COD account. I'll start by defining each of these.

Open Accounts

When you operate with an open account, you will have a credit limit based on your ability to pay as well as a set amount of time to pay your invoices. One of the main benefits of operating with this type of account is that when you order a roll of carpet for a client, you will have time to install the carpet and collect the balance before any money is due to the manufacturer. Time limits vary, but you will usually have ten to thirty days to pay the invoice. Some manufacturers will offer you terms—an additional discount, typically 2 to 5 percent, for paying the invoice early. That means that if your invoice in the amount of $1,000 is due thirty days from the date of invoice, and you have terms of 2/10/net 30, you may deduct 2 percent and owe only $980 if you pay the invoice within ten days, or you may take up to thirty days and pay the full balance. A terms discount can add up if you are doing $40,000 a month in invoices. (It would save you $800 a month; over a year it would total $9,600.) Terms are sometimes negotiable with your manufacturers, so be sure to call the credit department and ask. If you are on open terms with your manufacturer, be sure to protect your account at all costs. If you become delinquent on too many invoices, the credit manager won't hesitate to change your account to a COD account.

COD Accounts

If you set up a COD account, it will cost you additional money. If you ordered the same roll of carpet on a COD account, you would not only have to have the check ready when the product was delivered, you also would have to pay a COD fee. The fees vary with each company and product, but $5.00 is usually the minimum. Think how fast $5.00 can add up when you are receiving twenty deliveries a month ($100 x 12 months = $1,200 per year). Not only will you be paying the COD fees, but you also will not have the luxury of terms. If you add the lost savings from terms ($9,600 in our earlier example) to the added costs of the COD fees ($1,200), your business will be paying approximately $10,800 per year more than it has to.

The other disadvantage of having a COD account is that your money will be tied up until you collect the balance from your client. The one-half deposit that you collect from your client usually won't cover your entire cost of the job. If you sell a carpet job for $4,500 and your cost on the job is $3,000, you would have to come up with $750 of your own money to pay for the product when it's delivered because the one-half deposit is only $2,250. On certain types of jobs that have longer production times, such as shutters or draperies, your money may be tied up for weeks or even months.

Some of the smaller companies, such as local shutter manufacturers and drapery workrooms, may require that you give them a 50 percent deposit before they start the job, and then the balance would be due when the product is picked up. These are exceptions, but plan on having one or two accounts like this. You will usually get a better price and delivery time from small, local manufacturers.

When you first open your business, some manufacturers may set you up as a COD account on a trial basis. In those cases, if you prove yourself creditworthy (i.e., don't bounce any checks and pay the invoices on time), they will usually convert your account to an open one within about six months. Other manufacturers will give you an open account right at the beginning if your personal credit is good. That may be one of your deciding factors about whom you decide to do business with.

Credit and Your Clients

Some of your jobs will be large dollar amounts and your clients may need to finance the job. You can help them do this in various ways, and I will cover those options in this section.

Extending Credit through Your Business

Extending credit to your customers can be risky, so give it a great deal of thought before agreeing to do it. I had always refused to finance my clients, considering the risks too great. One time I was working with a couple who had just given birth to a child, and they began to run into financial difficulties halfway through the job. We were in the process of doing their entire house, one room at a time. They wanted to continue the job and asked me if I would consider financing the remainder of the job. Normally I would have begged off, but I had built a relationship with them over the months and felt I could trust them. I agreed, and we worked out a payment plan that consisted of four payments per section of job we would do. For instance, we did their living room at a cost of $4,000, and they paid me $1,000 per month for four months. This arrangement meant that I would have out-of-pocket expenses for the job for four months. We added a finance charge to the balance to cover my time and paperwork expenses and make up for any interest I would lose. Next we did the kitchen and worked out the same arrangement with that part of the job. In this case, extending credit was a successful option.

I don't recommend that you offer this option to everybody, however, especially when you are just starting out. You must have a healthy positive cash flow to sustain even one of these accounts. You also must realize that you are taking a risk: You can lose your money just as easily as you can collect it. You can reduce your chances of loss by running a credit check on your prospective clients, but even that's not entirely foolproof. For instance, another experience I had with this type of situation didn't have such a rosy ending. I was working with a very prominent family in the community, so the fact that they had a cash flow crisis in the middle of the job came as a surprise to me. They told me that their funds were tied up for a few weeks but if I could continue the job and wait to be paid, an agreed-upon percentage would be added to the final payment. Since the family was so well known in the community and the home I was designing was located in the most expensive part of the city, I felt I was taking little or no risk. I was wrong. I completed the job within a few weeks, but the payment didn't come. I called my clients several times and was always told that I would receive the payment within a matter of days. After a few weeks of this stalling, I realized I was in trouble. They stopped returning my phone calls and ignored my letters and invoices. I did eventually collect on the invoice a few months later, but only because the clients did not want to risk their reputation in the community. If they had not been so well recognized, I might have never collected on the job.

Using a Finance Company

There are easier and less risky ways to help your clients attain financing than extending credit through your business. If you look in the yellow pages under "Financing," you will find a collection of small finance companies. These companies will work with your clients in getting financing for their jobs. It's a good idea for you to research each company to find the one with the best interest rates, terms, and customer service, because when you refer your clients to one of these companies, they will most likely view it as an extension of your company. Some of these companies will offer financing for those customers who don't have a sparkling credit report, but keep in mind that the interest rates will be higher than the going market rate. The finance companies will also offer special terms such as ninety-day financing, one-year-same-as-cash, or even long-term financing.

Accepting Credit Cards

Accepting credit cards in your business is perhaps the easiest and best way to offer your customers credit. When I began to accept credit cards in my business, my sales went up substantially. If you think about it, most people use their credit cards to make major purchases, so it stands to reason that if they are buying $3,000 worth of carpet or blinds, they'll want to use their credit card and pay the balance in small monthly installments.

There are many credit-card processors out there who will try to sell you their services. They all represent the same companies: MasterCard, Visa, Discover, and American Express. The difference is the rates and services that they offer you. Let's start with the most basic item: the credit-card machine. Most of the processing companies will try to sell you a machine outright; those machines can cost from $850 to $3,000. What they won't tell you (unless you ask) is that they also have used equipment for sale at a substantially reduced cost. Another option is to lease the machine, but if you plan on being in the business for a long time, it's probably to your benefit to buy one outright. If your budget won't allow you to purchase a machine in the beginning, lease one with an option to buy. There are several variations of the machine.

- There is a fixed machine that sits by a phone line in your home or office, but it isn't very handy when you are on an appointment in your clients' home and they want to pay with their credit card. This machine will instantly give you a reference number if the card is approved. The funds will begin their journey to your account as soon as the transaction is complete.
- There is a more old-fashioned model that you manually operate by running a credit-card slip over an imprint of the credit card. The problem with this type of machine is that you can't verify whether or not the card is good or even check the credit limit at the crucial moment of the sale. Another problem is that you have to mail the credit-card receipt to the processing center in order for the funds to be deposited into your bank account. That usually can take anywhere from two to four weeks.
- Perhaps the best type of machine for this business is the mobile processing machine. It's compact and lightweight, so you can carry it into your customers' home and plug it right into their phone line. You will be able to verify the card right then, and the process that starts the funds on the way to your bank begins immediately. The funds can take one hour or three days to reach your bank, depending on the processor that you use.

The next and most important thing to look at is the rate the processing company offers you. When someone makes a purchase from you for $2,000 and uses a credit card, your processor is going to charge you a fee. I've seen fees range from 1.75 percent all the way up to 6 percent. A lot depends on your credit rating and the processor with which you decide to do business. If you use a processor that charges you 3 percent, your bank statement will show $1,940 on that $2,000 sale ($2,000 − 3% [$60] = $1,940). If you are paying a higher rate of 6 percent, your take from the sale just dropped to $1,880 ($2,000 − 6% [$120] = $1,880). You will usually pay a higher rate to accept the American Express card than the other credit cards. That's why American Express is not always accepted everywhere MasterCard, Visa, and Discover are.

It's illegal to add on the processor's charges to a sale to make up for the rates you have to pay, but no one says that you can't plan for it. If 60 percent of your sales are coming from credit-card sales, total the amount that you are paying in fees and work that into your overall selling prices. (Be sure to stay competitive.) Much of today's business is conducted with credit cards, and just because you are a small business doesn't mean that you shouldn't be in on it.

Now that your accounting system is set up, your accounts with the vendors are set up with either open or COD terms, and you have researched the various ways to help your customers finance their jobs, it's time to start setting up your files. I'll take you through the simple things such as bid sheets, invoices, and vendor files first, then we'll move into more complicated areas, such as customer contracts and the job tracking worksheet. I'll start with the bid sheet because that's the first piece of paperwork you will generate when you have contact with a customer.

Bid Sheets

You won't always close a deal with a customer the first time you meet with him or her. Sometimes it will take you three or four visits. In those instances you will need to leave a bid sheet detailing your bid. I will discuss the bid sheet and how to use it to sell in chapter 7, but an example of what a typical bid sheet looks like is shown on page 73.

Invoices

Up until the point when a customer commits to giving you a down payment, the only paperwork you will have are your notes pertaining to the customer's styles, colors, and measurements. You may have furniture style preferences or fabric swatches in a file with the customer's name on it, but as far as company paperwork goes, the invoice will be the beginning of the paper trail. You can buy preprinted generic invoices at any office supply store or have them customized with your company name and logo on them. Many large companies still use the preprinted invoices and purchase an inked stamp with their name, address, and

Sample Bid Sheet

Date _____

Customer _____

Address _____

Phone Number (Home) _____

Phone Number (Work) _____

Product _____

Rooms and Sizes_____

_____

Bid Price $ _____

Tax $ _____

Total Bid $ _____

Bid Good Until _____

phone number on it to personalize the invoice. I suggest that if you want to use custom invoices, wait a few months to determine what the best format will be for you.

Since this business is custom, there are various ways in which you can make the invoice work better for you. A four-part invoice works best because there will be many jobs where partial payment is made halfway through the job. Give the first copy to the customer on the day you accept the down payment, and put the rest of the copies in the client file that you have created. If you install half the job and you require payment for that portion of it, give the client the second copy after you have noted the second payment on the receipt. That leaves the third copy for the final payment receipt and the last copy for your file as a record of the transaction. On jobs that require more than one receipt, simply start a new receipt and write the number 2 in large, bold script on the upper right-hand corner. This will help

Typical Preprinted Invoice

Purchase Order No. _____

Customer Name _____

Address _____

Phone Number _____

Salesperson _____ Date Shipped _____ Shipped Via _____ F.O.B. _____ Terms _____

Quantity	Description	Unit Price	Amount

Subtotal $ _____

Tax $ _____

Total Due $ _____

Cost Plus Designs

1234 Money Street
Big Bucks, CA 12345
(777) 777–7777

Sample Custom Invoice

Date _____   Invoice No. _____

Cost Plus Window Coverings and Design

CUSTOM SERVICE AT DISCOUNT PRICES

1234 Money Street
Big Bucks, CA 12345
(777) 777–7777

Salesperson	P.O.#	Shipped Via	Terms	Estimated Delivery Date

Room	Quantity	Description	Unit Price	Amount

Subtotal $ _____

Sales Tax $ _____

Shipping $ _____

Total $ _____

Deposit Amount $ _____

Balance Due $ _____

All custom sales final—No returns or exchanges

Thank You!

you keep track of all the receipts for each job. Then you will enter the receipt information onto the job tracking worksheet that I will explain later in this chapter. On the following pages I have provided you an example of a typical preprinted invoice as well as an example of a custom invoice that may prove more useful for your interior design business.

Client Files

Because of all the information you will gather on each client and the amount of details you will have to remember, it's important that your client files be well maintained and organized. In them you will keep all the measurements, the fabric swatches and/or fabric names to be used on the job, time schedules for each project you're working on, and any special instructions. In addition to these details, you will keep the obvious client information on a sheet in the front of the file. Such information should include the client's name, address, phone number, type of work, product selections, method of payment, and so on. There is a sample copy of a client file sheet in this chapter.

In many cases, you will do work for a client on more than one occasion. You may design a bedspread and draperies for the master bedroom, and three months later you may be called back to wallpaper the kitchen or carpet the living room. I've worked with some clients for years. To keep the details straight, I usually staple the information for each part of the job together, with the client worksheet on top of it. Then I'll start another client worksheet for the next job. (All the worksheets should be kept in the same file.) The measurements and fabric selections will be loose in the file for the ongoing job.

We discussed earlier in this chapter why it's imperative to sign a contract with the client before starting any job. Now let's examine what to put in that contract.

The first section of the contract is where you determine who is who. This is where you will establish what everyone will be called and what the location of the job is. For instance, you can call your client the *homeowner,* and yourself the *contractor.* From there you will get into the more specific rules of the contract.

The first issue you should address in your contract is the fact that the order is a custom one. The customer should understand that with custom orders, returns and cancellations are not allowable. Once an order is placed and in progress, it can't be cancelled without penalties. If the customer decides to cancel the order before it's in production, you should still assign a fee (such as 10 percent of the order) as a *cancellation fee* to cover the time and expenses you have already put into the job.

Next, you need to protect yourself from the back orders and drops that will occur in your vendor lines. A *back order* occurs when the vendor you are ordering from has not received the product from the mill. A *drop* occurs when the mill decides to replace a style or color with one that it thinks will sell better. Once a product has been dropped, it is not available anymore. A simple statement relieving you of any obligation toward an exact delivery date is important to guard against delays caused by back orders and drops.

Flowchart of Product

Mill ⟶ Vendor ⟶ Retailer (You) ⟶ Customer

As a designer, you'll constantly be giving out advice on colors and styles. Sometimes clients will be unhappy when they see the final result, even after you have drawn the design and showed them the colors. But that is their responsibility, and the contract should state so. There can also be a problem with dye lots in some fabric, wallpaper, and carpet samples and with various wood products. With these samples, there is a possibility that the actual finished product will vary slightly in color. The contract should relieve you of any obligation in this regard as well.

Your returned-check charge should be stated in the contract. Find out what your bank will charge you if one of your customers gives you a bad check. Pass this fee along to the customer with $5.00 or $10.00 added to it for your time and expense in collecting it.

There will be times when customers will swear that they talked to you and you told them that you would add a free bedspread to their order, or they will make some other outrageous claim. Place a clause in the contract relieving you of any obligation for phone or verbal conversations, and this will alleviate the problem. You will be under obligation for only what is stated in writing in the contract.

A final suggestion for your contract is a clause stating that the prevailing party in a legal battle will be entitled to all costs and attorney fees. Such a provision will keep any clients from filing a frivolous lawsuit.

A sample contract follows on page 79; it is to be used only as an example. I suggest having an attorney look at it and add anything pertinent to your area.

Job Tracking Worksheet

This is perhaps one of the most important tools that you will use in your business. It will help you keep track of your customers and their orders, whether or not you have been paid, the estimated delivery date, the date of installation, the date the invoice is due to the vendor or contractor, and when it was paid. It will tell you how much commission is due to your employees, how much the contractor labor amounted to, and more. If you have a computer, you can run your weekly, monthly, and even yearly totals with a couple of keystrokes. Even if you don't have a computer, I highly recommend using this sheet and filling in the blanks manually.

What follows, on page 80, is the worksheet I designed for my business—out of frustration because the ones on the market simply did not address the specific needs of a custom-order business. With this system, you can list each specific order of the job separately. If you want to pull up the entire job file on your computer, simply type in the sidemark, and everything relating to that customer's name will appear. I have provided a sample copy of the worksheet entries, and I'll go over each of these column headers in detail and explain what each abbreviation means and how to fill in the blanks (see pages 81–83).

Sample Customer Contract

On this the _____ day of _____ , _____ , Cost Plus Window Coverings and

Design (contractor) enters a contract with _____

(homeowner) to do the following work at _____

_____

_____

_____

_____

The following terms and conditions apply to the above-mentioned work.

1. All details written on the invoice and signed by the contractor and homeowner shall become part of this contract. Any information given or received over the phone or verbally is not part of the contract.
2. All merchandise sold is custom product and cannot be returned once the order is in progress. If a cancellation does occur before the production of the order has started, the homeowner will be responsible for a 15 percent cancellation fee. This is to cover time and expenses.
3. There will be a $25 fee for any returned checks.
4. Homeowner is responsible for any color or style that is chosen. The decorator will help in the selection but assumes no responsibility for it.
5. Contractor is not responsible for any acts of nature or manufacturer back orders in relationship to product. The delivery dates assigned are estimates and depend on the availability of the product from the vendor. Contractor will not be liable for any delivery dates scheduled.
6. Certain products will show variances in color and grain. This is typical, and the contractor assumes no liability.
7. The prevailing party shall be entitled to all costs and legal fees in the event of any lawsuit filed by either contractor or homeowner.
8. Freight and installation are included in the total price only if stated on the invoice.

I have read and understand the above terms and conditions for doing business with Cost Plus Interiors. Any questions or concerns have been addressed before entering into this legally binding contract.

Date _____

_____   _____
Homeowner   Contractor

Sample Job Tracking Worksheet*

Cost Plus Interiors Job Tracking Worksheet

Date	P.O. #	Rep.	SM	Retail	Tax	Tot.	Dep.	Dt. Pd.	Bal. Due.	Dt. Pd.	Vendor	R.E. #	Op.	Del. Dt.*

* This chart represents the first fifteen columns of the forty columns I use. See pages 81–83 for an explanation of these and other column headings.

Cost Plus Interiors Job Tracking Worksheet

1. *Date.* Put the date of the order here.

2. *P.O. #.* Use the purchase order number from your invoice here.

3. *Rep.* This is the space where you will assign the job to a salesperson if you have employees.

4. *SM.* This is the sidemark, or the customer's last name.

5. *Retail.* This is the retail price before tax.

6. *Tax.* This area is for the total sales tax charged.

7. *Tot.* Combine the retail and sales tax here. This is the column you will use to total your sales figures.

8. *Dep.* Fill in the amount the customer gave you as a deposit.

9. *Dt. Pd.* This space is to record the date the customer paid the deposit.

10. *Bal. Due.* This is the amount the customer owes. You can record a second half of a deposit due here or a balance due from a customer you billed.

11. *Dt. Pd.* Record here the final payment date of the job.

12. *Vendor.* This is the manufacturer from whom you've ordered the product for the job. If you have more than one vendor per job, simply fill in the sidemark at the start of the line and skip to this section. *Do not* fill in the sales price and other data again because it will mess up your monthly and yearly figures.

13. *R.E. #* This is the reference number all vendors will give you when you place an order for product.

14. *Op.* This stands for *operator.* You should place here the name of the customer service person who took the order.

15. *Del. Dt.* This is the delivery date that is promised to you when you place the order.

Continued on next page

16. *Mini.* This and columns 17 through 30 are to be checked if the order contains one or more of the products. For instance, if an order contained twenty-four miniblinds, you would place a 24 in this column. At month's or year's end, you can total the product columns and determine what you are selling the most of and what you need to concentrate more on.

17. *Vrt.* Vertical blinds.

18. *PS.* Pleated shade.

19. *CP.* Crystal pleat.

20. *Wd.* Wood blind.

21. *Shu.* Shutter.

22. *Top.* Top treatment.

23. *Fab.* Cut fabric.

24. *Drp.* Custom draperies.

25. *Hdwr.* Drapery rods or hardware.

26. *Crpt.* Carpet.

27. *Wlpr.* Wallpaper.

28. *Tile.* Tile.

29. *Wd. Fl.* Wood flooring and related accessories.

30. *Misc.* Put any product not listed in columns 16 through 29. If you find that you are using a lot of a certain product not listed in those columns, add it to your worksheet with its own column.

31. *Cost.* Enter your cost of the product here.

32. *Inv. #.* Put the manufacturer's invoice number here. This will save you a lot of time when they call with questions about a specific invoice.

Continued on next page

33. *Pd.* Enter the date you paid the invoice.

34. *Inst. Dt.* The date the installation took place goes here.

35. *Inst. Amt.* Enter the amount you paid to the contractor to have the product installed.

36. *BB.* This stands for *buyback*. A buyback is any product that isn't salable to the customer. If you measure a window wrong and your cost of that blind is $23, it would go in this column. Most of the time the cost of these "Oops!" products are unrecoverable, so this column will be a total of your losses.

37. *Rbt.* Enter any rebates you get from manufacturers here.

38. *Cm.* Enter any commission paid here. You will use this column for referral fees and sales commissions.

39. *Dt. Pd.* Enter the date you paid these commissions.

40. *GP.* This is your estimated gross profit. Subtract all costs, commissions, installation charges, and buybacks from the sum of the retail plus rebate columns.

Chapter Six
Advertising on a Budget

Advertising Goals

When you operate a business out of your home, customers will not be walking in off the street to do business with you. People will not drive by your home and realize that there is a business inside. You must rely on unique ways of advertising to attract your potential customers. Advertising is the lifeblood of your business; it's what will bring you the sales that you need in order to have a prosperous business. Your goal should be to build up referral business so that in time you can reduce the costs of your advertising expenses, but in the beginning advertising is all you have to rely on. In this chapter I will discuss the typical advertising techniques that most businesses rely on as well as some alternative forms of advertising that are unique to the home-based interior design business. These alternative forms of advertising will also save you money while bringing in the much sought-after business. While some of the larger stores rely on big-dollar advertising forms such as newspaper and television, smaller home-based businesses generally don't have the budget to compete that way. That's where alternative advertising comes in. If you combine the typical advertising methods with the alternative ones in a consistent manner, you will soon have more business than you can handle.

Keep in mind that all the advertising in the world is not a substitute for good old-fashioned customer satisfaction. As I stated earlier, referral business is your goal; it decreases your advertising costs and increases your closing rate. (When a customer calls you from a referral, that person generally won't shop around because someone trusted has recommended your business.) Remember that referrals can work both ways. I once heard that if you do a good job you can count on that person telling three people, but if your work is unsatisfactory, they will tell ten people. That can mean the difference between "breaking in" to a new subdivision or not. Through good referrals, I have done work on almost every house on a block. But by the same token, on the rare occasion that I had an unsatisfied customer, I was rarely invited back to any house on that block.

In summary, advertising is the way to get appointments so that you can sell your products, but customer service and satisfaction is the method in which you will build your business into a long-term profitable venture.

Before We Get Started . . .

I will be referring to *free in-home estimates* throughout this chapter, so this seems like a good place to define what that means. When you advertise a free in-home estimate, you are making a promise to your customers that whether they buy from you or not, you will come to their home and give them an estimate for whatever work it is that they need done. A free in-home estimate is something used to attract business. Almost every one of your competitors will offer them, so if you don't, it could hurt your business. When you are invited to enter a customer's home to give a bid, your chances of making a sale go up drastically. When a customer sees a great-looking fabric swatch laid out over the worn-out sofa or a carpet square in the perfect shade of blue thrown over the stained brown carpet, it increases the chance of a sale. I have always used the technique of free in-home estimates to promote my business, and I will use it for examples throughout this chapter.

Typical Advertising Techniques

Yellow-Page Ad Placement

Some businesses rely a great deal on the yellow-page advertisements that they place in the phone book once a year. Some company names are designed around getting the best placement in the yellow pages. For instance, have you ever noticed names like AAA Appliances, or Advantage Lawn Mowing in the phone book? With those types of companies, being first is important because that's how a lot of people choose those types of services. The interior design business is different. Can you imagine choosing a designer that goes by the name of

ABC Design? Most people choose the name of their interior designer by the sound of the company name. We talked about this in the section of the book dedicated to the naming of your business. What impression do you want people to have of your business when they look at your ad? Do you want them to know that you are competitive in your pricing? If you want to emphasize window coverings as your specialty, make sure your ad states it. Following is a typical yellow-page ad.

Although you will be running an interior design business, you will get most of your calls from yellow-page categories other than interior design. You don't have to use a large ad like the one in the example for every category. Pick the category from which you want to get most of your business. If you are specializing in window coverings, place your display ad under "Miniblinds" or "Draperies," and place line ads under the rest of the categories. (*Hint:* Unless you plan on opening a carpet store that stocks rolls of carpet, or a

COST PLUS WINDOW COVERINGS AND DESIGN

Custom service at discount prices!

Miniblinds • Carpet • Verticals • Wood floors/tile
Draperies • Wallpaper • Shutters • Reupholstery
Residential/Commercial

Call Today for a Free In-Home Estimate!
777–7777

VISA   MasterCard

wallpaper store that carries hundreds of wallpaper rolls, I don't recommend purchasing a large ad for these categories. Those markets are very competitive, and as a home-based business you will be overlooked by most consumers. Window coverings and upholstery are the easiest products to promote from a home-based business because the price structure is set up so that a small business can be just as competitive as a larger one. You will get the carpet and wallpaper sales as a result of doing a total package for your customer.) Some of the other areas you may want to consider placing an ad in are miniblinds, vertical blinds, shutters, draperies, venetian blinds, window coverings, reupholstery, and of course interior design. The categories in each city will vary slightly, so go through your local phone book and determine in which ones you should advertise. Also make sure you pay close attention to the categories that your competition advertises in, especially the companies that have been around for a while. They have already gone through the trials and errors of advertising, so follow their lead. If you can't afford to advertise in all these categories, choose the ones that best fit your business and advertise there.

You might be able to negotiate one or two yellow-page line ads for free if you pay for a display ad, and you shouldn't have to pay for your line ad in the white pages. There are special deals that you should ask about and take advantage of. One year the yellow-page sales office offered me one-fourth off the regular price of my ad if I would specify what area of town I usually worked in. No problem; the top of my ad read "Northwest," but I placed the words "Serving All of San Antonio" on the next line.

Next, you will need to determine what points you want to stress in your ad. Obviously, your business name and telephone number should be in large bold type, but since your name won't be your biggest selling point, place it at the bottom. If you plan to offer any special deals, such as a free in-home estimate, this information should also be in large bold type. Avoid using your address: You don't want potential customers ringing the doorbell while you're in the middle of cleaning the kitchen floor. You will want to offer a list of all the services you plan on offering and include such wording as "competitive bidding" or "lowest prices offered." Some of the manufacturers you work with may offer a quick turn-around on certain products; if so, promote that fast service in your ad. If you plan to accept credit cards in your business, display the appropriate symbols at the bottom of your ad. The yellow-page office will have *slicks* (reproducible designs) of these, or your credit-card processing company can provide them.

When you are satisfied with the *copy* (wording) of your ad, turn it in to your sales representative, who will give it to the layout department to assimilate it in the form of an ad. You will be offered a proof of the ad before you sign the final acceptance contract. Be sure to take advantage of this option. A few years ago I decided I was too busy so I skipped it, relying on the layout department to make my ad look good. When the phone book came out the next year, there was a dark, black box in place of the picture of the cute little window with the miniblinds that I had designed. Learn from my mistake: Your yellow-page ad is just too important to your business to trust it with anyone else.

Finally, here is a checklist you should go over when planning to advertise in the yellow pages:

- All of your important products and services are mentioned.
- Any special offerings, such as rush deliveries, are mentioned.
- Your company name and phone number are in large, bold letters.
- You have excluded your home address.
- You have included any credit-card slicks that are appropriate.
- You have offered a free in-home estimate.
- You have checked your major competitors and made a list of the most-often-used categories.
- You have placed your company name in as many categories as you can afford.
- You have requested a proof of the ad before signing the final acceptance contract.

Business Cards

Another traditional form of advertising is business cards. Pass them out to anyone and everyone who will accept them. Pin them up on community bulletin boards, leave them lying on restaurant tables, and include them with all your correspondence. Business cards are also one of the least expensive ways of getting your business name in the public eye. If you decide to join one of the associations that I mentioned in chapter 2, plan to take your cards with you to meetings and hand them out.

Designing your business cards is just as important as designing your yellow-page ad. It should include the important information about your business without looking too crowded. Because of the nature of your business, you can take chances with your cards: the more creative, the better. Your business cards will be a statement of your style. If you have decided that your company colors will be blue and gray, make sure your cards reflect that. If you are going to design a logo for your business, use that on your cards too. Anything that people will recognize as yours will help with name recognition. Extend these ideas to your business stationery, contractor shirts, magnetic car signs, and so on. Make sure everything carries the same theme. As your business grows and you begin to advertise, more people will start to recognize your name. I remember the first time someone told me that they had heard of my business—it was a wonderful feeling! Another one of my customers told me she had seen my name on a billboard over the highway, and that's what made her call me. I had never advertised on a billboard sign next to a highway, but that made me realize that my name recognition was growing. It doesn't matter where customers think they saw your name, as long as they remember it.

The things that you will want to include on your business cards are the name of your business, your phone number, fax number if applicable, e-mail address, Web site address, your name and title, and what services you provide. Leave off your home address. I think it's a good idea to include the offer of a free in-home estimate again.

You will have many different choices when it comes time to purchase your business cards. There are some inexpensive cards that will cost you approximately $30 for five hundred cards, but if you decide to go with color and use a logo, your cards will run much more. Keep in mind your specific situation. If you don't have a lot of start-up capital, buy the inexpensive cards for the first year, then upgrade as you start to make money. An example of a typical business card follows.

Newspaper Advertising

If you are planning to advertise in the newspaper, you must make a long-term commitment to it. Running an ad once or twice is not going to bring you much business; it will mostly be a waste of money and effort. Newspaper advertising can be expensive depending on where you live. In most of the larger cities, the cost of advertising in one of the large newspapers is usually out of the question for most home-based businesses.

There are plenty of different options out there. There are lots of "shoppers" on the market. These are newspapers designed for the average person looking for used equipment or services at a discount. If you are planning to push a lot of window coverings, carpet, wallpaper, or upholstery, this is an ideal place to get the word out. Keep in mind that customers calling you from one of these ads will be looking for a bargain. This is where the loss-leader theory comes in. You can advertise miniblinds at a substantial discount, but once you get into the customer's home, you can suggest more profitable items such as verticals or shutters. (See the section dedicated to up-selling.) The idea is to get into the home and build a relationship with the customer. Only then can you make your best sale.

Another option for print advertising is the community newspapers or newsletters. Some subdivisions or small communities will have a newsletter dedicated to the issues of their community. They will use it to promote community garage sales, holiday events, and their homeowners' association news. They also sell advertising space in their newsletters very inexpensively. If you live in one of these communities, you should absolutely be advertising in that newsletter, but you can also advertise in the ones for communities that you don't live in. Look in your yellow pages under "Associations," or contact a few real estate offices to find out which communities offer such newsletters. I have been in almost every community newsletter in my city and have reaped quite a bit of business for a minimal investment. When you place an ad in one of these newsletters, make a special offer to that community. If you are advertising in the Oakwood Farms subdivision, your ad might look something like the one on the next page.

Television and Radio

Television advertising is expensive if you advertise in a time slot when people are watching. I recommend that you avoid using this form of advertising; it's just too expensive and won't

Sample Community Newsletter Advertisement

Special Offer for

Oakwood Farms Residents

75% Off Miniblinds!! • 60% Off Vertical Blinds!!
10% Off Drapery Fabrics!! • 20% Off Upholstery Fabrics!!
Free Lining with Any Custom Drapery Purchase!!

Cost Plus Window Coverings and Design Interiors

777–7777

Call Today for a Free In-Home Estimate!!

produce the kinds of results that other, less expensive forms of advertising will. Radio advertising is also questionable. It's hard to track your results from radio because a lot of people won't even remember where they heard your name. Radio is good for name recognition if it's used over an extended period of time, but for immediate results, stick to something that will cost less and bring you better results.

Mailing Lists

You can purchase a mailing list from a list broker by whatever category you choose. (Look in the yellow pages under "Mailing" for a listing.) The list brokers offer lists by income, subdivisions, even by people who have recently bought a new home. I've always found that the new homeowners list produces the best results. (You can also specify a price range.) These lists usually include the names of the homeowners, their address and phone number, the date of purchase, and even the purchase price of the home. You can use this information in two ways: (1) by mailing them information about your services, or (2) by calling them directly and trying to set up a free in-home estimate.

If you decide to mail the target customers information, be aware that the response rate is approximately 1–2 percent. Don't mail expensive color brochures or something that will require a lot of postage. Some of your manufacturers will sell color photo postcards that you can personalize by adding your company name and phone number. This is a great way to get an eye-catching color postcard at a substantially reduced cost. These postcards usually have pictures of room settings showing off a specific product, such as shutters or wood flooring. The postcards are a good-quality item that you can mail out with relatively little expense. (If you went to a printer and had the postcards made up yourself, you would probably spend at least triple the amount that these will cost.) On the back of the postcard is where you should promote any sales or other special offers. The purpose of a direct-mail piece is to catch the attention of the recipient and make her or him want to call you. It will help if you put a time restriction on the sale because that will create a sense of urgency for the potential customer. There are many different holidays and seasons that you can use for reasons to have sales. Some of the manufacturers will produce postcards that are specifically geared toward a holiday or season.

The other way you can use the mailing list is to call new homeowners directly. This approach works best if you call in the evening hours, when you will catch more people at home. Your goal during this phone call will be to set up a free in-home estimate. Explain to the homeowners that you understand that they have just purchased a home and you might have some products and services that they could use. Make your offer of a free estimate and if they accept, set up the appointment right then and there. Be prepared with all of your price lists and a calculator when you make these calls, because some of the people will want price quotes on the spot.

Billboards

If you can find a billboard located in a high-traffic residential area for a reasonable price, grab it. Billboard advertising is a great way to get your name known in the marketplace. If you offer an enticing sale on the billboard, that's even better. The problem is, most of the

Telemarketing Checklist

1. Have the information in front of you, and try to make the call personal. For example, is the customer remodeling or building a new home? Have you done work in their neighborhood? If so, tell them about it, and mention their neighbor's name as a referral.

2. Have a script handy that outlines the points you want to cover, but don't read from it. You want to sound like a capable professional who's able to solve their interior design needs—not an hourly worker who's paid to read a script.

3. Have a goal. Whether it's scheduling an appointment or getting permission to call again as the house is closer to completion, you should always have a purpose for the call.

4. Make an offer. Why should this person listen to you? You must make them an enticing offer in the beginning of the phone conversation, such as a discount or free installation, to draw them in. Otherwise, you're just another pesky salesperson.

5. Respect their wants. There's nothing worse than a pushy telemarketer. If they don't want to talk to you, thank them for their time, and hang up the phone.

6. Follow up. If you don't set an appointment, but the person sounded interested, send them a brochure, sales flyer, business card, and a personal letter thanking them for their time. If you don't hear back within a few weeks, follow up with another phone call.

billboards are located next to highways or other high-profile areas and are just too expensive. There are different sizes of billboards, and logically the smaller ones are less expensive. Keep your eyes out for the one that you think might be right for you. If you are lucky enough to find one, design the ad with bright eye-catching colors (yellow and red are great) and make an irresistible sales offer on it. Keep the copy in the ad simple and make sure your name and phone number are in bold, large print. Remember that your potential customers will be driving by in cars and won't have time to write down all the information right then.

Bench Ads

Have you ever noticed the ads that are displayed on the backs of benches? Such bench ads are an affordable, effective way to get your name in the public eye. There are different types of bench-ad plans available; prices vary depending on how many benches you advertise on at one time. If you display your ad on only one bench, you will pay more for that ad than if you were to advertise on five benches at once, because then you would be entitled to a volume discount. Another reason to advertise on more than one bench at a time is that you will have to pay a one-time layout fee for the layout design of your ad. The price will be the same whether you use it for one bench or ten. After that fee, the monthly advertising rates are fairly inexpensive. Use the same layout techniques that you would use on a billboard: Keep it bright and simple.

Magnetic Car Signs

This is another way of advertising unless you are a maniac driver who will promote bad feelings about your company among the other drivers. Simply go to a sign shop and order two magnetic signs to place on the side doors of your car. They should also be brief and to the point. Some people have a problem with this type of advertising because it could possibly put you in a vulnerable position. I have to admit, I stopped using these signs after a few years because I received some disturbing crank phone calls. Not only are you exposing your business to the public, but they are getting a glance at *you*, too (along with your phone number). If this possibility doesn't disturb you, it is an inexpensive way to put your business name in the public eye.

Brochures

Brochures are an excellent way to promote your business. Usually in color, they are designed with the idea of selling the products and services you have to offer. Unless you have a desktop publishing program and a laser printer, you will likely pay about $1,500 for a quality brochure. Some manufacturers offer brochures, but they only promote that manufacturer's products and are generally too generic. As your business grows and it is in the budget, a brochure can be a useful form of advertising. When you call on new-home Realtors, some of them will let you leave brochures on a counter in one of the model homes. Brochures are also a great marketing tool for commercial clients or high-end residential clients. When calling on architects, remodelers, or Realtors, a quality brochure will make a solid first impression.

Associations and Networking

I mentioned associations in the previous chapter, but they are so important I think it would be helpful to mention them again. Go to as many meetings as you can and pass out your business cards. Make deals with people. I once set up an arrangement with a large water softener company (that business is booming in my area). The water softener salespeople also market new subdivisions very aggressively, so we exchanged a stack of business cards. We handed out each other's cards whenever we were asked for a referral for that type of business (and sometimes even when we weren't). The system worked quite well—we both got a lot of business that we probably wouldn't have gotten otherwise. The point of this story is this: Don't go to these meetings and just stand around waiting for something to happen. Remember the reason you are there: to increase your business. Network, and watch your business grow.

Alternative Advertising

Now we'll discuss some ways to advertise your home-based interior design business that are less obvious but highly effective.

Door Hangers

Pay attention to this section because it's one of the least expensive ways of advertising and it can bring the greatest results. This technique works best in track home subdivisions that are relatively new (there are usually a lot of new homes being built at one time in this type of area). Design a flyer, or *door hanger,* including the name of your business, your phone number, and a sales promotion that will catch the attention of the recipient. Take it to a

Spring into Savings with a Free In-Home Estimate!!

Miniblinds 75% off

Shades 55% off

Draperies 20% off

Carpet $12.99/yd.

Upholstery 30% off

Wallpaper 2 for 1

Cost Plus Window Coverings and Design Interiors

777-7777

Custom Service at Discount Prices

Call before April 1st and receive free installation!!

printer and have them do the layout work for you. There will be a flat fee for this work, and the cost can run anywhere from $25 on up depending on the amount of work. For the example flyer I have provided, I would expect the layout costs to run $25 to $40. If you have a computer with a laser printer, you can do the layout work yourself, saving money. Then you can buy a ream of brightly colored paper and make the copies yourself, which will save you a great amount of money. (I've always received the best response from fluorescent yellow.) Then drive to a new subdivision, park the car, and hang one of these flyers on every single door in the subdivision. I usually spend two entire days per month and cover every new subdivision in the city. (It takes a full day to cover the entire city, and I do that twice a month.) It costs approximately $80 a month, between gas and printing costs plus my time, but I get a huge response. When you consider that the average cost of a job is $734, and I get ten jobs a month from this form of advertising alone, I'd say it's well worth the time. Change the look of the ad every couple of months just to keep it interesting. Be persistent. If you are promoting window coverings and you have put a flyer on a particular home two times but they still don't have anything covering their windows, keep putting flyers on their door until they do. I have attained many jobs after leaving several flyers. There are two other things you can do while you are in a new neighborhood. I will cover both of these in the next section. Use my example of a door hanger as the basis for yours; it's been tried and proven successful.

Door-to-Door Soliciting

Granted, this method is not for everyone, but if you have the patience and motivation, it will increase your business. In new neighborhoods, most of the people moving in will need at least one of your products. They will be looking through newspaper ads and shopping around for the best deals, so why not make them an offer in person? Some people will be annoyed, but you will also talk to some people who are open to receiving a bid from you. While you are in a neighborhood passing out door hangers and you notice a home in need of your services, don't just drop the flyer off—ring the bell and hand it to the occupants personally. It will be unlikely that you will sell them on the spot, but you will make a contact. They may not want to set up an appointment with you right then, but if you make a good professional impression, they will remember you when they are ready to make their purchase. There is always a chance that they will set up an appointment then or, better yet, ask you to give them an estimate on the spot.

The first drapery job I did came from passing out flyers. There was a large home that had nothing on the windows and a man standing out front watering the yard. I walked up and handed him the flyer, then turned around and started making my way down the street. He called out to me to come back. Then he went inside, got his wife, and asked me to give them an estimate on the spot. I walked away with a $3,000 job, one I might not have had if I'd just left the flyer on the door.

Marketing On-Site Realtors

Another thing you can do while you're in the subdivision is build up your relationships with the on-site Realtors. An on-site Realtor is one who sits in a model home in a new neighborhood and waits for home buyers to come in and look at the houses. You can generate *referral business* from these Realtors, and that is absolutely the best type of business you can get. Here's how it works. Make up referral cards (see the sample at the end of this section) and pass them out to the Realtors. Explain to them that by handing out these cards to their customers, it will entitle the home buyers to receive a free in-home estimate (or whatever else you choose to offer). There will be a place on the card that specifies which Realtor passed out the card; this is important because there is usually more than one Realtor working at each subdivision. If a referral calls you and you sell anything, that Realtor will be paid a *referral fee*. You can offer Realtors a percentage of the sale or design a pay scale. For example, you can pay them $25 for every $1,000 in sales. If a job totaled $4,000, you would pay the Realtor $100. There are quite a few Realtors who have made money in the hundreds of dollars from me by simply passing out my cards.

Of course, in order for the Realtors to feel comfortable passing out your cards, you have to build up a relationship of trust with them. The Realtor who gave me the largest amount of business was the hardest to persuade to do business with me. It took months and months before he actually agreed to even discuss the possibility. Before he agreed to pass out my cards, he had a few requirements that he wanted me to meet. He asked me to submit sample price quotes using the measurements from each of his model homes. I also had to agree to let him know before any price increases would be put into effect. This may sound like a lot of proving oneself and hard work, but within three years this Realtor had sent me well over a hundred jobs. After some time, he was promoted to sales manager for the builder that he worked for, and our association continued. He and I worked a deal with the builder wherein I provided blinds for homes that weren't selling in order to increase the marketability of those homes. A few years later I took that builder on as a color selection account and also designed all of their model homes. Had I thought that the Realtor was asking too much of me, or had I not wanted to go to all of that trouble, my relationship with the Realtor and the builder might never have gone so far.

Treat every Realtor with the same consideration because this is a fast-moving business—the Realtor you give lousy service to today may be the sales manager tomorrow. In most cases, Realtors will give you a "test" job, and if the customer is satisfied with your work and prices, they will start giving you more referrals. Keep in mind that it's to their benefit to recommend a company with the best prices and service because if you do the job, they get paid too.

Once you develop a relationship with a Realtor, it doesn't end there. Remember, your competitors will constantly be trying to talk your Realtors into switching their business to their company. I usually spend another two days per month marketing new Realtors and visiting my existing ones. I occasionally will take my top producers doughnuts for breakfast or sandwiches for lunch. During the holidays, I take them all coffee cups (with my logo on them, of course!) filled with red and green chocolates. Anything to make them remember me helps. If I find that I'm too busy to visit them one month, I will at least make a phone call and say hello. Don't get in the habit of making phone calls every month, though, because you can bet on the fact that your competitors will be there in person. I have also found that if I'm having a slow month I'll call a few of my busiest Realtors and ask them for leads. When I explain to them that I'm having a slow month, they are always more than willing to oblige. (But don't overdo this technique—they'll get suspicious if every other month is a slow one for you.)

Another thing to remember is that Realtors talk to each other. If you are doing a good job for their clients, they will spread the word and additional business will come your way. If you do bad work, you not only will lose that Realtor's business, but word will get around not to use you. Another good thing about referral business is that the customer probably won't shop around; you will usually leave from the estimate with an order and a check. This type of business is to be protected at all costs. If a customer has a problem and you don't think it's your fault, you may want to consider eating the costs of the repair anyway. I'm not saying that you should let the customers walk all over you, but keep in mind what you have at stake.

Sample Referral Card

Cost Plus Window Covering and Design Interiors

Present this card for a free estimate.

777–7777

Referred by:_____

Related Professional Marketing

There are other professionals who can send you business besides on-site Realtors. You can also market architects, remodelers, and Realtors who sell existing homes. They are not quite as accessible because they are usually in an office guarded by a receptionist. One way to get through to them is to establish a friendly rapport with the receptionist. That person usually has more power than you might think; she or he can make sure your information gets to the appropriate parties or even schedule an appointment for you. But if treated rudely, a receptionist could relate that behavior to your target client or simply not pass along your information.

Another way to meet this type of client is through associations. I have met people through associations and then been invited to give lectures at one of their sales meetings on new products that the market has to offer. (A speaker at a monthly meeting is something they are always looking for, so make yourself available.) At the end of the meeting, pass out something for them to remember you by. Notepads or coffee cups with your name and phone number on them are good.

You should also be persistent when cold-calling a potential account. Leave a brochure and card the first time you visit, then call and make sure they got it. Call and try to set up appointments with the manager of the office. Explain that you would like to offer your services to the office; tell the manager about your products and services. If you get a meeting, write a thank-you note afterwards. If you haven't received any calls in three weeks, call them back and remind them of what you can do for them and their clients.

One more way to endear yourself to these potential clients is to be willing to tackle emergency jobs that other companies won't want to touch. Perhaps a vertical blind needs repairing, and your profit on the job would be only $15. Most companies would beg off, claiming that their schedule was full. Take the job, and the next one sent your way may be a lot more substantial. They will appreciate your helping them out of a bind and will remember you the next time they have a job to send someone's way.

Job Site Signs

Once you complete a job in a neighborhood, you can leave a sign in the front yard letting all the other neighbors know of your work. You can have these foam board signs made up for approximately $30 to $50 each. If you order a dozen or so at once, your costs will go down. This is a good form of advertising because neighbors talk, and a sign in the front yard is definitely a conversation piece. You will have to ask your clients' permission to leave the sign in their yard, of course, and if they agree, leave it for only a week or two. I've only had one problem when using these signs: my competition. Competition is fierce in my area, and my yard signs would always disappear in the middle of the night. Hopefully, your area competition won't be as unscrupulous, because yard signs can be an inexpensive way of letting all of your clients' neighbors know your name.

Contractor Shirts

When anyone representing your company goes to one of your clients' homes, they should dress professionally. You can promote your company image by requiring that your contractors wear work shirts with your company name, logo, and phone number on them. You should provide each worker with two shirts in case one of them gets dirty. The shirts can be T-shirts or collared shirts; just make sure they are neat and have your company name and phone number in large, bold letters on them.

Newsletter

If you have a computer, a newsletter—either in printed form or via e-mail—can be an inexpensive way to get the word out to your existing clients of upcoming sales and promotions. An added benefit is that your clients will probably pass along any coupons to friends who are in need of your services. Along with the sales promotions, include the latest information on colors, trends, and new products. Perhaps your existing clients will find a reason to do more business with you.

Home Shows

Once or twice a year in every major U.S. city, there is a home show held in the local convention center. If your city isn't large enough to have a home show, you can bet that something similar to it will be held at one of the local shopping malls. A home show is an event where retailers, such as yourself, show off their wares. They rent spaces in booths and set up displays that they hope will make the shoppers want to do business with them. There are many sizes of booths to choose from, and they vary greatly in cost. I have usually opted for a 10-foot-square booth, and that has always served me fine. One year, I got ambitious and rented one of the largest booths at the show. I went to great expense to hire models and use only the best displays. While I did well financially at the show, it just didn't justify the amount of time and money I had to put into it. After that I went back to my 10-by-10-foot booths and have rented that size every year since. You don't have to put a lot of money into your displays, but make sure they are eye-catching. They should encourage the shoppers to stop at your booth to find out what you have to offer. Plan to spend about $3,000 for a 10-by-10-foot floor space. Additionally, you'll have to construct a booth and buy a carpet for the floor and a sign for the top of the booth. Add in your marketing materials (brochures, etc.) and you'll probably have to spend about $4,000 to $5,000.

The great thing about home shows is that almost everyone there is looking for something for their home. There are also a lot of people there who are in the process of building

Trade Show Tips

- Have a dry run. Set up your booth in your garage or backyard and invite friends, family, and even good customers to preview it and give you suggestions.
- Have everyone working the booth dress the same. This will give your booth a more uniform, professional look. By using T-shirts with catchy phrases, you'll stand out in the crowd.
- Think high, not wide. Trade shows are usually held in large convention centers, and it's easy to get lost among the hundreds of booths, but even the smallest exhibitors can get noticed by building their booth up. Do this by purchasing the tallest back drape you can, and then adding a sign or banner on top of that.
- If you have employees, prepare them. Take the same stance as the dry run on your booth. Make sure they know their goals—setting appointments, getting people to register for the giveaway, etc. Role-playing can be an effective way to ensure that everyone knows his or her job.
- Perform frequent demonstrations at your booth to attract a crowd. Then draw them in with your knowledge and charm!
- Put plenty of chairs in your booth. Shoppers have been on their feet all day, why not let them sit in your booth? (I've even seen one carpet company offer foot massages to weary shoppers.)

a new home. Your goal once again is to set up as many in-home appointments as you can. Do this by offering a one-time sale good only for people who set up an appointment *at the show*. Another promotional idea is to hold a drawing at the end of the show and have people register for it. Give away a miniblind or some other product that won't cost you too much money but is something that the recipient will appreciate. On the registration form, ask for their name, address, and phone number. Once the home show is over, you should have set up as many appointments as you could. You will be extremely busy for the next couple of weeks, and your sales should increase drastically.

You will have a lot of new leads in addition to the appointments that you set up. Everyone who registered for your giveaway prize filled out a form leaving you with their name, address, and phone number. It will be tempting to let them sit until you have finished with your appointments, but don't. The people who registered for your prizes also registered with your competitors; don't let them beat you to the sale. Call these leads as early as the day after the show. It might be a good idea to offer them a postshow sale, such as an additional discount if they set up an appointment with you. Some of the people may be in the process of building a new home and may not be ready to set up an appointment. In that situation, you should agree on a date when you will call them back. Write it down in your appointment book and make sure you call.

Depending on how booked your schedule is, you may have to work more hours just before and after the trade show. Don't block out a segment of time for your trade show leads, because you risk losing some of your regular business. Try to squeeze in as many of your regular appointments as you can before the show begins.

Parade of Homes

Most communities put on a parade of homes show once a year. It's something like a mini home show, but instead of being held in a large convention-style area, it is held in a new subdivision. The builders who are involved in the show design and build their best homes. The builders will hire designers to make the homes look their best. Once you have been in business for a few years, you can start to go after this type of work, but in the meantime there will be booths available for rent just like at the home show. The difference is that the booths are located outside the homes, lining the street. I have rented booths in a few of the parade of homes events, and they can be just as costly as the home show, but you usually won't get as much traffic. If you have to choose between the parade of homes and the home show, I would recommend choosing the home show.

Fabric Parties

This idea will work best if you are living in a new subdivision, but it can be used in an existing one as well. Some fabric manufacturers will offer discontinued fabrics at a substantially lower price. There are limited quantities of these fabrics, and they don't last very long. Arrange with your sales rep to have a "showing" of these fabrics on a particular day. Then send invitations to all the homeowners in your neighborhood (you can get the list from the homeowners' association or a list broker) and announce the deal that will be offered on the fabrics. You will be amazed at how many people will come. Not only will you sell a lot of fabric yardage, you will probably get a few design jobs, too. When the fabric comes in, who will make the draperies and bedspreads that it was ordered for? Make sure everyone knows that you handle that part of the job too. You can hand out brochures at the party that detail the type of work that you do. That may spark some interest in the other services that you offer, such as wallpaper or reupholstery.

Advertising on the Internet

Depending on whether you use your Web site to sell products or just display your company information, you may or may not want to use the following forms of advertising:

- *Newsletters via e-mail.* This can be an inexpensive way to keep in touch with your current customers as well as any people who have visited your site and asked for more information. Send out a newsletter once every two months or so, and include your latest sales and product information. It's a good idea to include "referral deals" in your newsletter—offers that will reward your existing customers for referring you. (This will ensure that your newsletter is passed along.)
- *E-mail advertisements.* Another inexpensive way to keep in touch with existing clients, or to market to new ones, is to send targeted e-mails that contain specific offers on your products. Be sure to have consumers sign up on your Web site to receive these e-mails, or you may be accused of sending "spam"! (Hint: If you are sending out mass e-mails, it's a good idea to have an autoresponder set up so that any inquires are answered immediately.)
- *Banner ads.* Exchanging banner links with other like business (that aren't competitors) will increase the number of visitors to your site. For instance, you may exchange links with a landscaping company because both it and yours are companies that attract new homeowners. But be careful about placing too many banners on your site, because you want the consumer to see your product, not just a bunch of flashing banners. Also, thoroughly research every organization that you represent on your site, because they will be a direct reflection of you and your company. (Likewise, don't agree to advertise your company on a Web site that doesn't meet your standards.)

- *Write articles.* By writing and submitting articles about your specialty, you will become known as an expert in the field, and that can only increase your business. You can submit these articles to other like sites, targeted *E-zines* (on-line magazines that appeal to homeowners) or attach them to your own site. (Hint: If you write an article for your own site, be sure to submit it separately to the search engines. This way, when consumers search with keyword "shutters," they will be shown a link to your article, which should include a link to your Web site.)
- *Search engine placement.* A lot has been written on the subject of how to get ranked at the top of search engines. The problem is that most search engines have different rules for placement, and they change quite frequently. If you're serious about the Internet contributing largely to your business, you might consider hiring a search engine placement specialist. (Type in keyword "search engine placement" in an engine such as Google to see hundreds of options.)
- *E-zines.* A good way to accumulate a large e-mail mailing list is to start an e-zine about your subject—interior design. By offering relevant articles about colors and design trends on a weekly or monthly basis, you'll soon create a loyal following. Of course, in each issue, your products and services will be highlighted, along with other advertisers (who pay to be there). This method takes a lot of work and patience, but if done right, it can pay off handsomely.

Other Ways to Get Business

Reading the Newspaper

This isn't exactly a form of advertising, but it is a way to get business. There are lots of government jobs out there, and most of the time you will see an ad in the local newspaper telling of government intentions to do improvements on a certain property. The government accepts bids on all its potential jobs and usually grants the job to the lowest bidder. (Sometimes companies are ruled out because of poor business practices in the past or some other reason.) I discovered this avenue for business one Sunday while I was thumbing through the paper. I spotted an ad run by my city government in the classified section. The ad stated the city's intentions of reupholstering all the furniture in one particularly large building and requested bidders. I called the next day and was told there would be a group bidding that Thursday. I showed up, along with about ten other people, and was shown all the furniture that was to be reupholstered. Then they described the type of fabric they were looking for and told us that we had one week to get back to them with our bids and fabric swatches. I worked up a bid and got a cutting of the fabric I planned to use and submitted it to the appropriate person. A few days later I got a phone call informing me that I had won the bid. All from reading the newspaper—how easy can it get?

Becoming an Expert

You can become an expert in a variety of ways. One of them is to send press releases to newspapers and radio stations every time you or your business accomplishes a goal. This goal could include anything from completing a job at a local business to hiring a new employee. You should definitely send one out announcing your grand opening.

Holding seminars about your specialty will certainly put you in the public eye. If you become a specialist at window coverings, hold a seminar on no-sew swags. Let the word out that you are available for speeches at the local design program (and then issue a press release) or volunteer to write a design column in your local or community newspaper.

Seminar Tips

- Rent a meeting room at a hotel or motel to achieve a professional atmosphere.
- Advertise and plan weeks earlier. Put on a mock seminar for friends and family, and take suggestions on how it could be more fun and educational.
- Offer the seminar for free, and then offer a special discount to anyone who sets an appointment that day.
- Provide simple refreshments. You want the attendees to be comfortable.
- Have product on site to sell. For example, if you are demonstrating no-sew swags, have the drapery hardware there to sell.
- Be high energy, and make it fun. You'll probably do more of these, and you want the customers telling their friends about it.
- At the end of the seminar, hand out an anonymous critique. This will allow you to get honest feedback so you can improve each time.
- Keep track of sales so you'll know whether or not the seminar is bringing you enough sales to justify the effort.

Tracking Your Business

One of most important rules of advertising is to keep track of where your business comes from. I have listed a lot of different advertising methods, and I'm sure you will think of even more. Each community is different, and it's hard to tell which form of advertising will attract most of your business. If you use an advertising tracking system, there will be no guesswork involved, and you will save hundreds of advertising dollars every year. Whenever you get an inquiry call, whether it turns into a job or not, ask callers where they heard about you and then make a note of it in your advertising tracking log, a sample form of which follows. After a few months you will begin to see a trend.

Next, you will need to tabulate where your jobs are coming from. There is a section in the advertising tracking log titled "Jobs?" Write a yes in the space if the call turns into a job and no if it doesn't. When tabulating your results, keep in mind that it will tell you where the "shoppers" and the serious callers are coming from. If you've had thirty calls from one ad but only two of those people bought from you, you might not want to run that ad again. On the other hand, if you've had five calls from another ad and four out of those five people bought from you, that's an ad you will want to run again. Tracking isn't something that you should do only when just starting your business. Rather, it will help you plan and keep track of your advertising for the life of your business.

Using Existing Clients to Cultivate New Business

After a while, your largest source of new business will be sitting right there in your files: your former clients. Repeat business is a wonderful compliment to your business; it means someone liked your work enough to hire you again. When your former clients call you to do additional work for them, there is usually no bidding involved. You already have a relationship with these clients, and they trust you and your work.

Your former clients may not always call you, however; sometimes they may not even realize that they need to update their colors or styles. It's your job to remind them of that. There are several ways you can do so. The newsletter that you send out will be a constant reminder to your clients that you are consistently keeping up-to-date on new products and services. You can also make periodic phone calls, about every six months, just to find out if

Advertising Tracking Log

DATE _____ CUSTOMER _____

ADVERTISING SOURCE _____ JOB? _____

NOTES _____

DATE _____ CUSTOMER _____

ADVERTISING SOURCE _____ JOB? _____

NOTES _____

DATE _____ CUSTOMER _____

ADVERTISING SOURCE _____ JOB? _____

NOTES _____

DATE _____ CUSTOMER _____

ADVERTISING SOURCE _____ JOB? _____

NOTES _____

DATE _____ CUSTOMER _____

ADVERTISING SOURCE _____ JOB? _____

NOTES _____

DATE _____ CUSTOMER _____

ADVERTISING SOURCE _____ JOB? _____

NOTES _____

DATE _____ CUSTOMER _____

ADVERTISING SOURCE _____ JOB? _____

NOTES _____

they are in the market for anything. Holidays are a great time to remind them of your business: Send cards to all of your former and present clients. If you use one of the mail-order office supply companies, they offer customized cards at a fairly reasonable price. Handwrite every one of them—it will make a bigger impact. After sending out cards, my business usually experiences an increase. One more way to jog your former clients' memory is to send them an "anniversary" card on the date that your business started. Offer them a special "birthday" sale to celebrate this occasion.

Some of your former clients will sell their homes and move to new ones, or make additions or changes to their existing ones. By keeping in contact with these former clients, chances are good that they will call you to do additional work when that time comes.

One of the biggest reasons for keeping in touch with your old clients is the referrals that they can send you. They work in offices or stores and have friends and relatives; all of these people at one time or another will require your services. If asked enough times, your former clients will be an introduction to new clients.

One way to cultivate client referrals is to offer your existing clients something in return for sending you business. I have done this a couple of ways in my business. The first is to offer them a referral fee just like you do the Realtors. This can be fun if you tell them about the referral fee when you first write the contract and accept their down payment. I like to tell my clients that they have an opportunity to "work off" part of their balance. I let them know that for every person they refer to me who ends up buying from me, I will credit their account $25. Some of your clients will be enthusiastic about this prospect and work off a large portion of their balance. Think back to the average cost of a job ($734). If one of your clients sent you four referrals, your potential sales from that would be $2,936. Not bad for a $100 investment, eh?

The other way to entice your customers into passing out your cards is to offer them a discount on any work that they plan to do in the future. Give them a gift certificate (you can purchase these forms at any office supply store), and make your certificate in increments coordinating with the amount of business that they send you. For instance, give them a $25 gift certificate for every $1,000 that they send you in business. The advantage to using this system is that the gift certificates alone probably won't cover the cost of the future job. If they want to purchase $400 worth of wallpaper but have only $150 in gift certificates, they will owe you a balance of $250. You will likely still come out ahead.

After every job is finished, you should follow up with a thank-you note. It should be handwritten and personalized. This small gesture goes a long way in creating goodwill between you and your client. A few months later, send out a letter along with a few of your business cards, requesting referral business. I realize that you have already done this while you were still working on their job, but time has passed, and sending you business is probably not foremost on your customer's mind. For the cost of a postage stamp, your chances of getting another job are pretty good. On the next page there is a sample thank-you letter.

Keeping Track of Your Clients

This all sounds great, you say, but how do I keep track of all my old clients? It can be done several ways. If you have a computer, it's easy to start a client file, filing the names, addresses, and phone numbers alphabetically by last name. That will come in handy when you want to do something like mail out your newsletters: Simply transfer that file into your mail merge and your computer will print out your labels for you. If you don't own a computer, buy an expandable file folder or a large Rolodex and keep track of the names alphabetically.

In addition to the basic information, such as your clients' names, addresses, and phone numbers, you will want to keep track of the work done in their homes and any work that you know they may want done in the future. To keep an ongoing relationship with your clients, you'll also need to keep track of when and why you last had contact with them. This is the reason that I use the client tracking sheet. When you have completed a job and are ready to file the client folder away, staple the client tracking sheet to the outer front cover of the folder. (*Hint:* Staple it at the top and bottom to keep the sheet from tearing.) You want the sheet on the outside of the file folder because it will save you time when you are going through your files. You won't have to pull every one of them out and open them up; you can simply flip through them. Go through your files once a month to determine who needs a reminder of your services. Predetermine a period of time that should pass between phone calls or letters (six months in the beginning and once a year after that has always worked for me). Use the sample of the client tracking sheet that I have provided on page 114; it should prove helpful.

Sample Thank-you Letter

July 10, 2003

Cost Plus Window Coverings and Design Interiors
123 Anystreet
Anytown, USA 11111

Former Client
456 Anystreet
Anytown, USA 22222

Dear Former Client:

I wanted to thank you for your business once again. If I can be of service to you in the future, I hope you will not hesitate to call.

In the meantime, I have enclosed a few of my business cards. I would appreciate your passing them along to anyone in need of my services. As usual, I will mail you a referral fee for any business that comes my way due to your efforts.

I hope you are enjoying your new surroundings, and call me if I can be of any help.

Sincerely,

Suzanne DeWalt

Suzanne DeWalt

Sample Client Tracking Sheet

Name _____

Address _____

Phone number _____

Start date of job _____

End date of job _____

Work or service provided _____

_____

Work still to be done _____

Reason not done _____

Client satisfied with work? _____

Date of contact _____ Reason _____ Response _____

Date of contact _____ Reason _____ Response _____

Date of contact _____ Reason _____ Response _____

Date of contact _____ Reason _____ Response _____

Date of contact _____ Reason _____ Response _____

Date of contact _____ Reason _____ Response _____

Date of contact _____ Reason _____ Response _____

Date of contact _____ Reason _____ Response _____

Date of contact _____ Reason _____ Response _____

Date of contact _____ Reason _____ Response _____

Turning Inquiry Calls into Sales

When a person calls you on the phone with questions about pricing or services, that is an ideal opportunity for a sale. Again, your goal will be to determine what the person is looking for and then set up a free in-home estimate so that you can demonstrate how you plan to fill his or her needs. The first thing you will have to do is *qualify* the person, that is, determine whether or not the person is really ready to make a purchase. Some of the questions you may ask the caller are:

- How soon are you looking at having the work complete?
- Are you planning on doing work in one room or many?
- Have you determined a budget for this project?

If the caller has definite answers to these questions, that means that the person has thought it through and is probably ready to make a purchase. If the caller's answers aren't certain, he or she may just be shopping around. I have been surprised by people who I thought weren't really serious, however, so be courteous and helpful to all your callers. If your caller has answered the first round of questions confidently, then you will want to proceed by setting up an in-home estimate.

After you have established the time and place, you still need to ask this person a few more questions so that you will arrive at the appointment prepared. In addition to preparing you, those questions will also instill confidence in your prospective client by making the person feel as if you are taking his or her needs seriously and will work hard to fill them. The following questions would be appropriate if the caller was inquiring about draperies; adjust your questions appropriately according to the type of product that your caller is interested in.

- What room or rooms do you want draperies for?
- How many windows are involved?
- What is your style and color scheme? Do you want to change it or stay with it?
- Will you need new drapery rods or use the existing ones?
- Would you like for me to bring along coordinating upholstery fabrics or wallpaper?

- Are the draperies to be used for function or beauty? If beauty, do you also need to see some miniblinds, verticals, or shades?

By the time you hang up the phone, you will know whether the customer is interested in one balloon valance or a house full of draperies with a possibility of additional upholstery and cellular shade work. If you hadn't asked these questions, you might have shown up at the potential client's home with mostly contemporary fabrics and a miniblind sample only to discover that the person had been looking for a traditional rose print with white shutters, and you would not have made the sale. Use the phone calls as a way to establish a rapport with your client, and get the information you need to appear like the professional that you are.

Summary

Remember that along with your advertising efforts must come a service-oriented business that always puts the customer first. In today's competitive market a business cannot afford a bad reputation. Set the standard in your area for the highest-quality products, deliver in a reasonable time period, be competitive in your pricing, and put to use your newfound advertising ideas, and it will be hard for you not to have a successful business.

Chapter Seven
What to Charge

In chapter 1 we discussed the differences between a consultation designer and a product-oriented designer, whose profits largely come from the sale of products. We determined that the best way for new designers to set up a business is to use products as their main source of income. Because of the diversity of products and services that you can offer, pricing products and bidding jobs can get pretty confusing. I will show you step-by-step the process of determining your costs on the various products and services.

I will also take you step-by-step through the maze of giving a bid. There will be many times when you are asked to match or beat a competitor's bid. You will need to be able to take apart that competitive bid to determine what grade of product is being sold and for how much. For instance, what if a customer handed you a bid from a competitor for twenty-four miniblinds and asked you to match it? Before agreeing, you would first need to determine whether or not you could match it with the same product that you were bidding. If not, you would need to show the customer a less expensive product. There are literally hundreds of product manufacturers out there, each one selling different quality products for varying prices. A bid can always be matched; the trick is knowing how to do it.

It's also important for you to know your competitor's selling style. We will cover all these important issues in this chapter. I'll start with the process of getting to know your competition because that's the first thing you will be faced with on an appointment.

Shopping the Competition

If you are going to be successful in the home-based interior design business, you must know how your competition operates. You will have to know what their pricing structure is, what products they sell, what fabricators they buy from, who their employees are, when they have sales, and which market share they are concentrating on. Sure, you say, and how am I supposed to get all that information? The answer is research.

Your first step will be to determine which of the competitors are targeting your desired market area. If you live in a small town, your competition will probably be everyone advertising in the phone book and maybe even some of the businesses in the surrounding towns. If you live in a small city, you may share the market with five or six other similar businesses, and you'll have to get to know their way of doing business. If you live in a large metropolitan city, you may have thirty competitors, all concentrating on different areas of town, in which case you will need to determine which ones are concentrating on your targeted area and find out more information about those companies.

Once you have determined who your competition is, you will need to get more specific information. Looking in the yellow-page ads can give you a wealth of information. For instance, most companies will list the products that they sell. It's also a good idea to visit competitors' Web sites to determine their customer service policies, shipping time, and much more.

In their yellow-page ad, they will usually highlight their anchor product. For example, if they sell a lot of window coverings, that will stand out in their ad. Look for other clues into your competitors' makeup, such as their hours of operation, whether or not they accept credit cards, if they work out of a home or an office (people who work out of their homes usually don't list an address), the manufacturers that they represent, and any special offerings such as fast service or free in-home estimates. Use the worksheet provided on the next page to keep track of your competitors' prices and the manufacturers that they use. Fill out a separate worksheet for each competitor. Use a separate line on the sheet for each product. If they sell more than one type of blind, list each type separately.

From the sample advertisement that follows on page 120, you could determine that Bill's Home Emporium's focus product is window coverings and that Graber is his preferred manufacturer. He also probably gets co-op money from Graber—that is, Graber pays part of the cost for Bill's ad because it mentions Graber products, a technique called *cooperative*, or *co-op, advertising*. Bill's also sells a variety of other products. Bill obviously works out of his home and is probably a sole proprietor. He accepts all major credit cards. He offers a large discount on miniblinds while still promising a three-day delivery. No

Sample Competitor Worksheet

Name _____   Phone _____

Address_____   Target Area _____

Focus Product _____   Credit Cards? _____

In-House Installers?_____   Other Financing _____

Product	Manufacturers Used	Notes on Discounts Offered

Sample Competitor Advertisement

BILL'S HOME EMPORIUM

Miniblinds 70% off ★ *3-day delivery*

Vertical blinds	**Shutters**
Shades	**Draperies**
Carpet	**Wallpaper**
Upholstery	**Fabrics**

FEATURING GRABER PRODUCTS

555–5555

M/C   Visa   Discover

hours are listed, so he probably works around his clients' schedules. If you do this examination with each of your competitors, you will have the beginnings of your research.

The next thing you should do is to invite your competitors into your home and ask them to give you an estimate. Remember that most of your competition will offer free in-home estimates. Simply phone them and act like a potential customer in need of new draperies or carpet. They will bring their samples to your home and leave you with a bid for the products. Get bids on a variety of products: new carpet or other flooring, blinds and draperies, fabric and labor for reupholstering your sofa, and maybe even new wallpaper for your kitchen. Do this with each competitor you think you will bid against in the future. You not only will learn what products they are selling but what their pricing structure is as well. You also will get a glimpse of their professional style. Is one of them a high-pressure salesman? If so, that's something you should remember when you're bidding against him. Did another promote the fact that her installer is the best in the industry? Did they offer you financing? Will they negotiate their prices? How were they dressed? Did they have a professional manner? Ask them for their measurements and see how they react (more about this in the next chapter). Did they exhibit follow-through? Did they send you a follow-up let-ter? Did they call a few days after the appointment and lower the bid to get the business? All this information will tell you how your competition operates and put you ten steps ahead of the competition right from the start.

Don't feel bad about wasting your competitors' time because one day they'll do it to you. People in this business are constantly "shopping" one another. Once you establish a name for yourself and start taking away someone's market share, they will want to find out as much about you as they can. People who have been in the business for awhile may ask a friend or a neighbor to do the shopping because they are probably too recognizable. For instance, the larger manufacturers usually throw Christmas parties, and you will be wining and dining with your competition. (*Hint:* Don't have too many glasses of wine and say too much.)

Use this checklist to analyze your competition when you call them to your home for a bid:

- Were they organized? Did they remember everything that you asked them to bring?
- Were they on time?
- Were they dressed professionally?
- How long did they stay? Did they overstay their welcome or make you feel rushed?
- Were they knowledgeable about the products?
- Did you trust them? Did you feel confident in their abilities?
- How many times did they try to close you?
- Most important, if you had been a real buyer, would you have bought from them? If so, why? If not, why not?

Other Sources of Information

Another way to get valuable information is to talk to your manufacturers' representatives: They love to gossip. It's easy to throw out a question like, "So how's ol' So-and-so doing?" Amazingly, most representatives will tell you everything they know. They probably think that by doing this they will impress you with their knowledge or it will help create a professional relationship with you.

Yet another source of information is installers. If you use a contractor instead of a salaried employee, that contractor will be working for your competition as well. The installer will usually tell you who's keeping him or her busy and who isn't, and that in turn will tell you how much business the competition is doing.

One more person you may want to build a relationship with is the delivery driver. Some companies will ship the product to you with a company truck and their own driver rather than use UPS or some other commercial freight line. These drivers also go to ten or twenty of your competitors daily. They are a good gauge because they know who is receiving products and who isn't. If you hear that one of your competitors hasn't been receiving goods for a few weeks, you know that there is a problem.

While all these people are good sources of information, it's important to remember that if they talk to you, they'll also talk to your competition. It's a good idea not to tell them anything you don't want your competition to know. A representative once told me that my fiercest competitor told him she was considering getting out of the business; she said she was tired of it all and didn't feel like she was giving her customers quality service anymore. What a valuable piece of information to have! I quickly shifted my marketing efforts to the people from whom she received her referral business. Sure enough, they were getting complaints about her and gladly accepted my business cards. It wasn't long before I started receiving the referral business from them that she had been getting. (By the way, she didn't get out of the business, but as a result of telling her representative something too personal, she lost a good percentage of her business to me.)

The Bidding Process

Bidding on a job can be complicated and time-consuming, but it doesn't have to be that hard. Unlike many other businesses, this one uses the markup system. You will first need to determine the profit margin with which you are comfortable. You have already calculated your overhead costs, so now you have to take into consideration the cost of the product, the cost of your time, and the cost of any contract labor.

Make sure that you include all of the following in each of your bids:

- The cost of the product
- The cost of all labor (drapery workroom, installations, etc.)
- Your time and overhead
- Your markup
- Any additional materials

Figuring Product Costs

Determining the cost of the product is easy. We will start by learning how to calculate your costs on each type of product. Unfortunately, you will calculate your costs depending on the method the manufacturer uses, and most of them will be different. You will be given either wholesale lists or discounts to be applied to the retail price list from each manufacturer. I have included a sample of a wholesale price list from a carpet manufacturer below.

We will get into specific details of how to measure and figure yardage for carpet jobs in chapter 9 of this book, but for now let's imagine that we are bidding a job to carpet 100 yards of a house (when we say *yards*, we mean square yards). The price listed in the right-hand column is your cost. Now you need to add on labor, padding, and your profit on the carpet. For the purpose of this example, let's price labor at $4.00 per yard and padding at $3.00 per yard. (Be sure to check in your own area for the going rate.) Your customers are big spenders and decide on the Abloni carpet at $8.99 per yard. If you are comfortable with

Sample Wholesale Price List

ABC Carpet Company

Carpet Name	Fiber	Cost per Square Yard
Abloni	100% nylon	8.99
Bruzza	50% nylon, 50% olefin	5.99
Cantana	100% polyester	6.99
Delmar	100% olefin	7.00

a $3.00-per-yard profit on the carpet and a 25 percent markup on the labor, you would charge the customer $2,074.00 plus tax, as the following calculations show:

Price of Carpet (*cost plus profit*)	$8.99 + $3.00 = $11.99 per yard
Price of Labor and Pad (*cost plus markup*)	$7.00 + 25% = $8.75 per yard
Total Price per Yard	$11.99 + $8.75 = $20.74 per yard
Price for 100 Yards of Carpet	$20.74 x 100 = $2,074.00

Now let's look at the cost on that job. Your cost on the Abloni carpet is $8.99 and your cost on the labor and pad is $7.00. Your total cost on the materials and labor for this job is $15.99 per yard. If you take that figure and multiply it by 100 yards, you will get your total cost for the job, $1,599. You are selling the job for $2,074 and it is costing you $1,599, so your profit on the job is $475 ($2,074 − $1,599 = $475.00). Take a look at your overhead and the time you spent on the job. Is it worth it to you? If not, add another dollar or so per yard to the job if the market will bear it.

Now let's take a look at how to bid a job when you are working with a retail price list and dealer discounts. Let's imagine you are bidding on a vertical blind and the customer has a window size of 75 by 84 inches. The customer has chosen a vertical fabric named Mirage. I have included a sample of what a retail price list would look like. The retail price

Sample Retail Price List

Vertical Retail Price Chart (Mirage)

width	up to 24"	48"	56"	68"	80"	95"	104"
24"	48.00	60.00	80.00	100.00	120.00	150.00	210.00
48"	60.00	75.00	93.00	127.00	149.00	168.00	238.00
56"	89.00	96.00	110.00	139.00	162.00	179.00	249.00
68"	100.00	123.00	136.00	152.00	189.00	210.00	273.00
80"	122.00	140.00	153.00	173.00	199.00	256.00	310.00
95"	138.00	156.00	174.00	198.00	243.00	276.00	353.00
104"	156.00	177.00	190.00	233.00	276.00	299.00	397.00

of the Mirage vertical is $243. The way you determine that price is to find the width (75 inches) across the top of the price chart and then the length down the side (84 inches), rounding up to the numbers nearest yours. Thus, the price for your 75-by-84-inch blind would be the same as an 80-by-95-inch blind: $243.

The retail prices on these price charts are never the actual selling prices. Years ago retailers sold the product at list price, but the market has become too competitive. A standard sale for a vertical blind in my location is 60 percent off the retail price. (Be sure to check in your area.) That means you would sell the vertical blind to your customer for $97.20 plus tax and installation ($243.00 – 60% = $97.20). Here's where the discounts that you negotiate with your manufacturers' representatives are crucial. If you had negotiated a 50/50/25 discount, your cost for the vertical blind would be $45.57, figured this way:

Retail Price	$243.00
Less 50%	– $121.50
Subtotal	$121.50
Less 50%	– $ 60.75
Subtotal	$ 60.75
Less 25%	– $ 15.18
Discounted Cost	$ 45.57

Your profit margin on that blind would be $51.63, which translates to 54 percent. Supposed you had negotiated only a 50/10 discount, then your cost on the blind would be $109.35 and you would have to sell it for a lot more—$202.50—to make a 54 percent profit. Can you see how good discounts will enable you to be competitive in the marketplace? You will then need to add sales tax and an installation charge to your price. Later in this chapter I will explain how to hire a contract laborer and what to pay that person. I will also briefly cover sales tax and how to collect and pay it.

You will need to go through this routine with every product you sell. The easiest way to do it is to work backward. Look through the ads in your local newspaper, call your competitors out to give you estimates, and talk to those people with whom you are making contact to determine the price point you need to sell your products at to be competitive. Once you have determined that, you can work the numbers backward to arrive at an acceptable manufacturer's discount.

The last scenario I will cover is that of a designer working as a consultant. Shop the competition in the same manner that you did before, except this time you will want to get the information over the phone. All you need to know is the hourly design fee that the designers charge because in this situation there is no product sale involved. You should also ask them if they will offer a free one-hour consultation. An even easier way to get this information is to call up the design school in your area and ask what the going rate for a new designer is. Schools are usually more than willing to help you with any information.

Sample Product Price Sheet Chart

Wholesale Price List	Retail Price List with Discounts
Carpet	Window coverings
Drapery workroom labor	Fabrics
Installation labor	Wallpaper
Upholstery labor	

The Competitive Bid

As I've stated earlier, you will be asked to match competitors' bids on a routine basis. You must know how to dissect the bid in order to determine what product the competitor is selling so that you can then match the price. This will probably happen more times with the window covering products, so we'll use those as an example.

Avoid the Deep Discount Temptation

Before I talk about matching bids, there's an important point I need to make: Once you set your price, stick to it. Window coverings will probably be the largest portion of your product sales because you don't have to be a large store to get competitive pricing from the manufacturers. There are many people who will start a window covering business and sell the products for a small dollar amount over their cost. These people don't stay in business long, but there are always one or two popping up somewhere. Ignore them.

Of course there will be occasional exceptions to the rule of sticking to your price. You may be doing a large job and the customer asks you to do a small bedroom window at a discounted price. That's okay because you've probably made a good profit on the rest of the job. Let's say you have a customer you've been working with on designing her entire home. On the last room she fell in love with a fabric that cost $3.00 a yard over her budget. In a case like that, I'd probably lower the price of the fabric. As a general rule, however, don't give deep discounts. There will always be someone selling window coverings for less than you do. There is a market for that type of business, but I would advise you to stay away from it. You will work twice as hard for half the amount of money as someone who doesn't re-sort to deep discounts to make a sale. The best thing you can do for your business is to learn how to upgrade the products you sell, and we will discuss that in the next section. First, I'll teach you how to match a bid, product for product.

Matching a Competitor's Bid

There will be times when you will be asked to match or beat your competitors' bids. I'll start out with an example of a window covering sale. Let's say you have just given a bid for twenty-four high-quality miniblinds in a new home and your estimate is $2,100. You have built up a good rapport with the customer and you have high hopes that you will get the job. Just when you are pulling out the contract for her or him to sign, the customer whips out a bid from one of your competitors showing that they've bid the job for $1,700. Then the customer tells you that if you match the competitor's price, you can have the job. If you sold the same product you bid on for $2,100, your profits would instantly be reduced by $400. It's not likely that your competitor has bid the same product that low. Here's where your product knowledge comes in handy. Each manufacturer has about three grades of miniblinds: good, better, and best. If you come across a bid that is much lower than yours, it is probably based on a lower-grade product. If you have a copy of the competitive bid, it will make the comparison easier because you can then point out the name of the lower-grade blind to your client and adjust your bid appropriately. If you don't have a copy of the bid, you will have to try to explain the differences in the product to your customer. You should tell her or him that you would be happy to match the bid with the lower-grade blind; this way you are comparing bids product to product, price to price.

Let's go back to the Abloni carpet job that I talked about earlier. Say you just gave your bid of $2,074 for 100 yards to your customer, who then pulls out an estimate sheet from one of your competitors, Sam's Carpets. It seems that Sam is having a sale and bid the job at $19.74 per yard, bringing the price of the sale to $1,974. Your cost is still $1,599 on the job, so now your profit would drop from $475 to $375. At this point you need to decide whether the job is worth the lower profit.

One way you might overcome this problem is by showing the customer another product, one that you can use to match the bid while still staying true to your $3.00-per-yard markup. There are thousands of carpets on the market, so it shouldn't be too hard to find another one. But if the customer is definitely sold on that particular carpet, you have to make the decision then whether there is enough profit built into the job. (If you had researched the marketplace and knew your competitor was having a sale on that particular carpet, you probably wouldn't have shown it in the first place. You could have shown the customer another carpet that sold at the same price of the sale carpet and was equal in quality. This is just one example of how knowing your competition can put money in your pocket.)

Estimate or Bid?

The main difference between an estimate and a bid is that a bid is your final word. You may give an *estimate* (a rough price, subject to change) over the phone, but you should give a *bid* (a written promise to do the work for a specified amount of money) only *after* you have measured the house yourself and are confident that you have all of the pertinent information.

Up-Selling

Some people get into the bad habit of selling everything they have to offer at greatly discounted prices. By doing that you put your business in an unstable position because you have to sell twice as much as someone who doesn't give deep discounts; therefore when times are slow, your business will be in danger. You will have to advertise what is referred to as a *loss leader* in order to get the consumers' attention. A loss leader is a product that is advertised at a high discount in order to persuade consumers to call you. That's why miniblinds are sold at 70 percent off of the retail price and carpet is advertised for $6.99 per yard. But if you sold everything at that low of a profit, you wouldn't make enough money to support your business. The answer is to *up-sell*. There are better and more expensive products than the public is used to seeing. If you get to know these products, you can present them to your customer and increase your chances of a larger sale. For instance, if you sold a job of approximately eighteen wood blinds instead of the same number of miniblinds, you would stand to make a couple thousand dollars more on that one job. If you sold hardwood floors instead of carpet, you would also put a few thousand more dollars into your pocket.

Luckily, today's consumers have a better understanding of quality than did those of the past. There are still some people looking for the cheapest blinds or fabric to put on their walls, but that's okay—leave those jobs to your competitors. It's your responsibility to educate consumers about the choices they have. I usually take in samples of the best blind as well as the lowest-quality blind, or the best upholstery fabric and the low end. (The manufacturer can provide you with small working samples.) Once I show the customer the differences in the products and compare the costs, they will usually invest in the better-quality product. Even if they don't, I still feel as if I gave them a choice. Some designers will automatically bid on the lowest-priced product because they are afraid that if they try to up-sell, they will lose the job. Actually what happens is that the customer loses faith in them when their product doesn't hold up, and when they are ready to do additional work they will call someone else. That is no way to accumulate repeat business.

Another way to up-sell is to pay attention to the customers' needs. Do they have a sun problem? A miniblind won't keep out the heat, but a solar cellular shade will. Do they have children or pets? A silk fabric or wool carpet will only cause problems for them in the future. Too many salespeople are in the habit of telling the customers what they need and not paying attention to what the customers really want. You must learn to listen to what each customer is telling you. There's nothing that intrigues me more than a salesperson who automatically assumes that the customer is looking for the cheapest product. A lot of sales are lost that way because consumers' true needs are not being heard and, therefore, not met. Pay attention to their needs and you will automatically sell more expensive products.

Sales Tax and Your Bid

We talked about the basics of sales tax in chapter 2. You know that you will have to collect the required percentage for your state and make quarterly payments to the government. Some states do not require that you charge sales tax on labor. (Be sure to check with your local tax office.) In those cases you would charge tax only on the product that you sell and then add the installation charge after you've added the tax. If you live in one of these states, you can use the law to lower your bids. For example, if you sell a carpet job for $10,000 and $3,500 of that is labor, your bid would look like this:

Carpet and padding	$ 6,500.00
Tax @ 7%	+ $ 455.00
Subtotal	$ 6,955.00
Installation	+ $ 3,500.00
Total	$10,455.00

If you didn't know about the tax law, your bid would look like this:

Carpet, padding, and installation	$10,000.00
Tax @ 7%	+ $ 700.00
Total	$10,700.00

Contract Labor

Until you have built up enough business to hire full-time employees, most of your help will be on a contract-labor basis. A person who works as a contract laborer works for many companies; he or she is considered self-employed. For instance, the drapery workroom laborers who fabricate your custom draperies and bedding ensembles will work for many designers. At the end of the year, you will issue them a 1099 tax form instead of a W-2 form. You will not take any taxes out of their pay because they will be responsible for them. Some of the other people you will pay as contract labor include: carpet layers, wallpaper hangers, drapery workroom laborers, upholsterers, and window covering installers. One of your biggest challenges will be to find a good, reliable contractor for each of these areas. I'll suggest one method of going about it that worked for me.

When I first started out in business, I had no idea where to start looking for contractors. My first step was to call the various drapery workrooms and set up appointments with them. You can get the names of the workrooms from your drapery manufacturer representative or the yellow pages. There are usually some retailers listed in the "Drapery/Wholesale" section of the yellow pages along with the true wholesalers. Skip them; they are just trying to pass off as a wholesaler to the public. You can pick them out by expressions such as "wholesale directly to you" or other slogans directed toward the retail customer. True wholesale workrooms will generally say in their ad that they sell to the trade only. If you are in doubt, call them and pretend to be a retail customer who needs draperies and see whether they agree to bid on the job. Some of the best workrooms don't advertise because they get their business from word of mouth, so be sure to ask around. You will want to interview at least three because your rapport and work styles must be in sync. Make sure that the workroom you select is willing to work with a new designer. (*Hint:* Many workrooms will verify your yardage and labor estimates before you order the fabric. They will also look over your designs and alert you if there are any flaws in the design. Some workrooms will have a selection of drapery and upholstery fabrics that they will sell at their cost plus 10 or 20 percent. This service comes in handy, for example, when you are looking for an exact shade of yellow and you don't have it in any of your own sample books.)

When you meet with the people in the workrooms, pump them for information. They know who the best blind and drapery installers are; they may even put you in contact with them. They will have their favorite fabric manufacturers and will give you recommendations. They should also be able to give you contact names of wallpaper installers, upholsterers, and shutter manufacturers.

Once you've gotten all the information from the people at your drapery workroom, call each of the contacts they gave you and start asking the same questions. When you hear a company or a contract laborer mentioned two or three times, it's reasonably safe to use them for your jobs. The only person a workroom may not be able to recommend is a flooring installer (but it never hurts to ask). Ask the carpet manufacturers to give you a list of their recommended installers. Call each of them and ask them to send you a price list. Also ask them their fee for remeasuring a job for you. (I'll talk more about remeasuring later, in chapter 9, but it's very important that your flooring contractor be willing to do this.)

Scheduling Contract Labor

If you are using contract laborers, remember that their time is their own. It means that you have to plan ahead. Remember, they are working with five or six other designers, so you should schedule your installations as far in advance as you can. I keep an erasable board on the wall with the set installations on one side and the tentative installations on the other. If you are using contract labor, it's wise to have backup installers to call in case your main installer has another obligation when you need him or her. As you get busier and start giving the contractor more business, they will begin to put your needs ahead of people who don't give them as much business. (*Hint:* By using e-mail to communicate with your contractors, you'll save valuable time!)

Hiring Your Own Hourly Contractors

Keep this section in mind as your business starts to grow. You won't be able to implement this plan until you have enough work to keep the contractor busy full time. I think the best way to illustrate this concept is to do so with an example.

When I first started my business, I got some referrals from my sources for the various types of installers I needed. The window coverings installer charged an average of $3.00 per linear foot on the product that was to be installed. (This is an average of all the window covering products and in no way should be used as a guide.) That means that if I sold a job with two sliding glass doors (75 inches each) and twenty-five windows (35 inches each) there would be 85 linear feet to install. The installer's charge would be $255.00 for that job (85 linear feet x $3.00 per linear foot = $255.00). It wasn't long before I figured out that the people buying miniblinds and verticals weren't going to pay that kind of money. Sometimes I would have to absorb part of the installation charge in order to get the job. Drapery business is different. Custom draperies can be an expensive product, so another $10 to $30 per window usually won't matter.

I decided to hire a part-time employee and train the person to install the products. (Many manufacturers hold installation training seminars that you can attend and send your employees to at no charge.) I thought that if I paid an employee an hourly rate, my installation charges would go down. I paid my new employee $35 for the first hour on a job (that included a trip charge that covers gas and mileage) and $15 an hour after that. The same three-hour job that would have cost $255 using a contract installer would now cost approximately $65. The installation costs of that job just decreased by $190.

You can do the same thing with any type of installer. If you sell a lot of carpet, hire a full-time carpet installer; if wallpaper is your focus product, hire a wallpaper installer. Doing so will reduce not only your costs but also your bids, and, therefore, you will be awarded more jobs. Make sure you understand the installation process yourself before you try to hire anyone because you will need to answer any questions your workers have. You should get to know every aspect of your business anyway, and the installation process is no exception.

Payday

Most drapery workrooms will require that the balance is paid before the product is picked up. These are generally small companies that can't afford to extend credit. Most of your other contractors will want to be paid the day the job is completed. It's hard to keep control over the situation unless you are at each and every installation of every product you sell. Needless to say, that is impossible. I designed an installer job critique sheet that will help you alleviate some of these problems. The idea is that the contractor will fill out the sheet and hand it in to you along with his or her bill. You should never pay on a job without one. (Be sure to let them know *before* payday that that's how you operate.) The sheet will inform you of any problems that occurred on the job and what steps the installer has taken to correct them. For instance, if a vertical blind is 2 inches too short, has the contractor given you the correct measurement, room location, and exact window location? If not, that would mean you would have to make another trip out to the customer's home and remeasure the window yourself. I have included a sample of the installer critique sheet on the next page.

Installer Job Critique Sheet

SM _____   Date _____

Address _____

Product installed _____

Notes (If problems, include room or window location and nature of problem.)

_____

_____

_____

_____

Steps taken to correct problems

_____

_____

_____

_____

Installer's Name _____   Cust. Pd? _____

Installer's Signature _____

Amount of Invoice _____
(Attach copy)

An Inspirational Word

Don't be discouraged if after reading this far you don't feel like an expert. If you read this book and do all of the exercises, you will be well prepared for your first appointment. In the next chapter I will discuss the in-home estimate. The chapter following that will delve into product knowledge and give you specifics on measuring and figuring yardage. I have also included in that chapter some worksheets for you to practice with before actually going on an appointment.

Chapter Eight

Now That You Have an Appointment, What Do You Do?

Thus far everything in this book has prepared you for the appointment. You've set up your business legally, you've run your figures and prepared your business plan, and you know how much overhead you have and how much business you need to do in order to sustain your business. You have met with the various manufacturers' representatives and have decided which companies you are going to do business with. You've negotiated for the best sample prices and discounts possible, you have set up all of your files, and you've finally started to advertise. You handled your first estimate call aptly and turned it into an appointment for an in-home estimate. Right now, you're probably feeling a little nervous. It's time to take a look at what happens on a sales appointment. It's important that you take the lead from the beginning and stay in control throughout the appointment because that will better your chances for a sale. I will help you accomplish this by explaining what to expect. I'll give you hints and suggestions on how to handle various situations that may come up.

The first and largest section of the chapter will cover the appointment. I'll teach you the steps you need to take to increase your chances of a successful sale. I will walk you through an in-home estimate step-by-step, concentrating on the specifics of the sale. I will also touch on some basic selling skills. Be sure to read chapter 9 thoroughly and complete the practice worksheets before going to your appointment. The practice worksheets are full of examples making use of all the products that you will sell. You will be asked to calculate yardage and come up with solutions to tough measuring problems on the worksheets.

In the second section of this chapter, I will teach you what to do after the sale. You will have to order the product and make sure all of the contractors have what they need in order to complete their portion of the order. You will have to track the order, making sure that everything gets in on time, and handle any problems, such as back orders or flawed goods.

The third section of the chapter will explore the installation. It will be your responsibility to schedule the installation. I will tell you what to expect from the installer and give you some guidelines for when you should and shouldn't be at the installation. The chapter ends with a short final section on managing your sales.

The Appointment

Now let's examine the appointment. Your work begins well before you walk through the door of your prospective client's home.

Before the Appointment

When you set up the appointment over the phone, you should have asked the customer what type of work he or she was interested in doing. Once you found out the type of product the customer wanted to purchase, you should have asked some more specific questions (if you need a review, refer to the end of chapter 6). By doing so, you will have determined what samples to take with you on the appointment. Don't take too many samples because that tends to confuse the customer. It's your job to determine what products will best serve your customer. For instance, if the customer is interested in vertical blinds, you should take in samples from your preferred manufacturer but keep a different one in the car as a backup. Use it if the customer can't find anything she or he likes in the first sample book. The same idea applies to any product you are selling. If it's a carpet appointment and you have already established that the customer wants a Berber, carry in three different Berbers from a high, middle, and low price range. Keep a few more Berber samples in the car in case the customer doesn't find anything pleasing in the ones you carry in.

Make sure you have a price list for every product you take with you. You should also have price lists for all the other products that you sell, because if something comes up that you hadn't expected, you will need to give the customer an estimate. Besides your samples, you will also want to take along a tape measure, calculator, pens and pencils, appointment book, notebook, graph paper, customer contracts, and invoices. Use the notebook to record the measurements and the graph paper to draw the room diagram for carpet or the design of the window if it's complicated.

I've always found it helpful to get specific directions to the customer's house or office while you are on the phone. Most people won't mind taking the few extra minutes required to give you directions. In addition to that, I always carry a map with me in case I get lost. (The customer's directions aren't always perfect.) It's important to remember that you must be on time to your appointments—*always*. First impressions are the key to successful sales, and you won't make a good one by being late. Showing up late will put you at an immediate disadvantage because you will start the appointment by having to explain and excuse yourself.

Arriving at the Appointment

After you arrive on time and introduce yourself, start building a rapport with the customer. Some people will be getting more than one bid, so you will want to leave a good lasting impression with them. There is an old saying: "People buy from people they like." I have always found it to be true. There are others who claim that some people will pay more money to work with someone they trust. Ideally, you want both. You should strive to make customers feel comfortable with you and let them know that you are looking out for their best interests. One of the easiest ways to do that is by building a rapport with them. Do this by first talking about small things; maybe they have the same color scheme as you do, or perhaps they have a collection of sailboats that interests you.

After you have established a satisfactory rapport, you should ask for a tour of the room or rooms that the customer intends to work on. Take a mental inventory of the styles and colors in each room, noting any additional suggestions that you can mention later. For instance, if the customer wants to change the color of the draperies in the study, be sure to write down the color of any furniture in that room. If the new color doesn't match it, they might be open to reupholstering instead of buying new furniture. The same principle applies to bedrooms; does your client realize that you can also provide bedspreads, wallpaper, and carpet to go with the new draperies?

Next, you should sit down with your client and look at the sample books to determine what textures and colors appeal to her or him. The client already may have decided on the desired colors. In that case you should pinpoint the textures and styles the clients are drawn to. For instance, some people are drawn to the shiny, smooth texture of chintz fabric while others are drawn to the rough look and feel of a textured cotton. Many people have a hard time verbalizing their preferences, so ask them to look through a few magazines or your portfolio and point out which styles they like. From your phone conversation you probably have determined the budget for the project. Confirm this now and you can steer your customer toward the products that will fit into their budget while keeping their specific needs in mind. Your desired goal for this portion of the sale is to determine your client's color preference, style, and intended budget. After you have helped the customer make the selections, you will need to measure so you can quote prices.

Measuring

Up until this point you haven't been able to quote any prices because you haven't yet measured any of the floors, walls, or windows. This is where the appointment can start to get tricky. We will discuss the actual process for measuring the specific products in chapter 9, but for now we will discuss the general rules. I want to stress the importance of being able to concentrate while you measure. You will come across many situations where you will seriously need to ponder the measurements. Measuring will rarely be cut-and-dried. Sometimes there will be kinks thrown in, such as molding around windows or odd-shaped rooms or walls. Surprisingly, the biggest threat to your concentration is your customer. Most people don't understand the concentration level that it requires to think a job through, so many of them will follow you around and talk while you are trying to measure. As you will learn in chapter 9, the difference of merely an eighth of an inch in some products will determine whether or not it will fit. That's why it's important that you keep the customer occupied with something else while you measure. There are at least two ways you can do this.

The first way to keep your customer occupied is to assign him or her a task. For instance, if the customer is completely redesigning a room and you've already determined what flooring and fabrics she or he likes, leave the customer with the vertical blind book or drapery fabric samples and pictures to look through while you measure. This strategy will not only allow you to measure without interruption, it will also give the client time to visualize what you've already talked about and get excited about the idea.

If you are measuring for only one product, you will not be able to use that strategy because you have already selected the fabrics with the customer in order to build a rapport. For instance, if the customer called you to give her or him an estimate for off-white verticals throughout the house, all you would have to do is measure the house and pick out the vertical fabric. You wouldn't want to walk in, hand the customer the sample book, and start measuring because you wouldn't build any type of rapport that way, leaving the customer to base the decision entirely on price. If your competitor had given an estimate the day before and had taken time to build a rapport, the customer would probably feel more comfortable giving the job to her or him.

The way to handle this situation is with a video. You should first sit down with the customer and look at the vertical book together. Spend time with the client and build a rapport. When it comes time for you to measure the windows, pull out your window coverings video and plug it into the customer's VCR. Most of the manufacturers that you'll work with have videos for sale that highlight their products. These videos are usually fifteen or twenty minutes long, just about the amount of time you need to measure a house. All the videos are different, depending on what product they highlight. In the case of the vertical blinds video, the presentation will focus on the features and benefits of a vertical blind. The videos are well produced and will make you look even more professional.

But what if your client has no VCR? Your video won't be much use then. Fortunately, some of the manufacturers also sell well-produced, full-colored picture books that highlight their products. Most of the drapery hardware companies will provide you with a book full of photographs that show different uses for their products. These books are great sources for pictures of drapery styles. The flooring manufacturers also have many types of sales tools, such as books and brochures. You can also put together one of these books yourself. Look for magazine pictures and promotional literature that you receive from your various manufacturers and compile your own book. This way all the products you sell will be highlighted in one book. Your customer may see something that he or she hadn't thought of, and that could increase your sale. Use your imagination and think of different ways to keep your customer occupied while you measure for the products.

Pricing

There are two schools of thought on bidding. Some designers like to give the client a price during the first appointment because they think it will increase the chance for a sale. They figure that the client is excited about everything you've shown and to leave without quoting a price will break the momentum and give the client time to reconsider. On the other hand, some designers feel that they can't concentrate enough to work up a bid without making mistakes. Some bids can get very complicated, and it would take pure silence to work on them—not the best environment for building rapport.

I subscribe to the first theory. In my experience the chance of closing the sale goes up considerably if you can present the bid to the client during the first appointment. I usually tell the customer that I need about twenty minutes of quiet time in order to work up the bid. Most people are happy to oblige and will leave you alone, but some people won't stop talking and will make it impossible to concentrate. In those situations you will have no choice but to tell them that you will call later that day with a bid. There will be other times when you simply don't have an answer to a question that would directly affect the price of a bid. At those times you also will have to call the client back with a bid if you can't reach anyone by phone to answer your question.

Having said all that, I still don't recommend that you attempt to give bids on the first couple of appointments that you go on. Wait until you feel comfortable enough with the products and pricing structures. Again, make sure that you've practiced with the pricing worksheets in chapter 9 before you attempt to give a bid. Be sure to use the measuring guidelines that I provide in chapter 9 for each of the main products that you sell.

One thing you will have to be wary of is giving your measurements to the customer. There will be some customers who will try to take advantage of the free in-home estimate. They think that you will come measure their windows and then hand them the measurements or tell them how many rolls of wallpaper and border that they need at the end of the appointment. Then they will go to a home design store armed with your hard-earned measurements and purchase the products off the rack. The way to avoid this situation is to charge for the measurements. If a customer insists on having the measurements, simply tell him or her that you will be happy to sell them for $50.00 (or whatever you think your time was worth). Let the customer know that if he or she buys from you, the amount will be deducted from your bill. This policy might make some customers angry, but it's the only way you can assure that your time is not being wasted. Remember, you promised a free in-home estimate for your products and services, not a free measuring job.

The Close

The close is obviously the most important step in selling the job. Everything you have done up to this point has been in preparation for this moment. Show your client the bid and explain that the price includes labor, materials, installation, and tax. Don't give a breakdown of the price unless the client asks for it because that will do one of two things: It will make it easier for the client to shop around and compare your prices, or it may just confuse them.

If the customer decides to and compare your bid with the competition, it will be easy for them to beat the bid by showing a less expensive product. If it's a drapery job that they are comparing, they will know from your breakdown that you are charging $25.00 per yard for the fabric, $15.00 per width for labor, and $3.00 per foot for installation, so all they have to do is bid a $20.00-per-yard fabric to beat your bid. The same applies to all of your products. You want to make it as difficult as possible for your competitor to break down your bid.

When a customer buys a product, she or he usually thinks of it in terms of a finished product. If you break down a carpet bid and show the individual prices for the carpet, padding, tack strips, installation, and disposal of the old carpet, you are only asking for trouble. The customer will see all the different prices and feel as though it's costing more than if you had just given one figure.

During your presentation of the bid, take note of your client's expression. If the client's face registers a shocked look, she or he has probably not priced custom products before. Explain the quality that they will be getting for the money. Ask for the client's thoughts. If they feel that the price is a little out of range, make alternative suggestions to bring down the price. (This is where product knowledge is crucial.) But if the client was nodding approvingly throughout the presentation, that is your cue to pull out the contract and ask for the deposit.

Sales 101

Unfortunately, a lot of designers believe that if they are good with colors and have a flair for design, the jobs will automatically fall into their lap. Not true. You must be good at sales as well in order to be successful in this business. I highly recommend that you take some time to read a book on sales techniques or attend a class, but I'll take a few moments now to explain the basic rules.

1. *Assume that you already have the sale.* Your attitude will come across as you interact with the client; make sure that it's a confident one. From the moment you walk in the door up until the time you pull out the contract, assume that you are there to write up the order.
2. *Make sure that you are talking to the decision maker.* It's very frustrating to spend a couple of hours with a client selling the design of a room only to hear the words, "I'll have to discuss it with my husband," or "I'll have to talk it over with my wife." It's a good idea to schedule the appointment when both the husband and the wife will be at home if it takes both of them to make a decision.
3. *Sell the features and benefits of a product instead of the product itself.* Everyone you bid against will be selling the same product that you are. If you relate the fact that hardwood floors will increase the value of a home, it will mean more to your clients than simply pointing out how beautiful wood floors are (they already know that).
4. *Sell your company, but don't trash your competition.* My internal red flag goes up when someone I'm buying from starts talking badly about one of his or her competitors. People who feel the need to denigrate their competition are probably trying to overcome some of their own shortcomings. Such behavior is viewed as unprofessional and will usually create negative feelings.

You will face many customer objections in the course of an appointment. It's your job as the designer to listen to the objections and either counter them or find another product that will suit their needs. After you have handled all the objections your customer has brought up, you will need to attempt a trial close. The purpose of a trial close is to tell you whether or not you're on the right track with the sale. I will use the following dialogues to demonstrate this technique, first with a window covering sale and then with a carpet sale.

CUSTOMER: *I love the beautiful wood look of the shutters you've shown me for my windows, but the price is way over my budget. I guess I'll have to wait until I can save enough money. Thank you for your time.*

YOU: *Mrs. Jones, did you realize that my company accepts all major credit cards and even offers interest-free financing through a company that I work closely with?*

CUSTOMER: *Yes I did, but my husband and I never use credit. We feel that if we can't afford it, we don't really need it.*

YOU: *That's a smart way to live, Mrs. Jones. Tell me, how much were you expecting to pay for the shutters?*

CUSTOMER: *About half of what you've just quoted me.*

YOU: *I see. Most people don't realize how much custom shutters cost. Did you realize that wood blinds are available in 2- and 3-inch slats and would give you the same beautiful wood look as the shutters? The price of wood blinds is beautiful, too—they run about half the price of shutters!*

CUSTOMER: *I didn't realize that. Do you have a sample you can show me?*

YOU: *Absolutely. I'll get them out of the car. Would you also like for me to bring in a contract in case you like the look as much as the shutters?*

If your customer answers yes to that question, you have successfully overcome all of her objections. If she says no, you'll have to keep digging to find out what her real objection is. Then you will have to overcome that and try to close her again. Now let's suppose Mrs. Jones wants carpet.

CUSTOMER: *I like the color and style of the carpet, but I'm afraid that the light color will show stains.*

YOU: *Mrs. Jones, you have selected a carpet that gives you a ten-year warranty for stain protection. The carpet is a blend of Olefin and Nylon; these fibers are*

extremely stain-resistant. The color will achieve the light and airy look you
want for the resell value. You get it all in this carpet: style, color, and excellent
stain protection. Now would you like to proceed with this carpet?

CUSTOMER: *But what about installation? How can I be sure that it will be done right?*
YOU: *I use a carpet installer who has been in the business for fifteen years. I'd*
be happy to give you the names and phone numbers of a few of my clients
as referrals.

CUSTOMER: *That would be great. I know it would put my husband's mind at ease. Now*
tell me about the financing you offer.
YOU: *Of course we accept all major credit cards, but I can also work with ABC*
Financing Company to help you get six-month financing same-as-cash.

CUSTOMER: *That sounds like what we need.*
YOU: *Great! Why don't we fill out the credit application and write up the order?*

Again, if the customer agrees, you've sold her on the product. If not, you still have
work to do.

Before You Leave

Make sure you have recorded all the measurements and information pertinent to the sale,
such as fabric names and colors, the best time for installation, and any special items relating to the job. It would be embarrassing to have to go back later and remeasure or recon-
firm a fabric choice. Write down all this information on the contract, being as specific as
you can. Also write down the total selling price and note how much deposit was paid. Ask
your customer to sign the contract. Once the paperwork has been taken care of, it's time to
leave. Hand the customer a business card and explain that you will call with a more definite delivery date once the order for the materials has been placed. Answer any last-minute
questions and leave on a positive note.

One of the most commonly heard complaints about designers is lack of follow-
through. Call your client within a day or two and confirm an estimated delivery date. It's a

good idea to call the client at least once during the production time to give an update. It may seem like a great effort, but this little bit of goodwill goes a long way. Remember, this customer could lead to another one—provided that you give fair, honest service.

Three-Day Right of Rescission

In most states there is a law that gives customers the right to cancel any order that was sold to them in their home within three days. This law will apply to you. You will have some tough choices to make because most of the jobs you get will be based on the speed of delivery. If you wait the three days before you order, that will add three days to your delivery time. If you don't wait the three days and order the product, you are taking a chance. Let's say that a customer ordered miniblinds for her entire house and needed them immediately. You didn't wait three days before ordering, and the customer called you on the second day and canceled the order. Most manufacturers ship out miniblinds the second or third day after you place the order. In this case the blinds could have been shipped, and you would have had to absorb the charge. (Remember, custom products are not returnable.) Yet if you had waited the three days and quoted the customer a six-day delivery instead of a three-day delivery, you might not have received the order in the first place. You will have to use your instinct on each individual job. If time isn't an issue to the customer, by all means wait the three days before you order any products.

If They Didn't Buy at the Appointment

You've done your best. You put together a beautiful color package that compliments the room. You've sold them on your designs. They appeared interested, shaking their heads yes throughout the presentation. When you handed them the bid, they thanked you for your time. You explained to them the options they had (credit cards, financing), but they remained vague. They said they would call you and walked you to the door. As you loaded up your car, you tried to figure out what went wrong.

You will ponder this type of situation may times in your career. Believe it or not, some people will just use you to get ideas; some don't realize how expensive custom products are. Some people may not have enough money and have poor credit. Others are just bored, and a free in-home estimate sounds like a fun way to spend an afternoon. The most probable explanation is that these customers are getting more than one bid. In that case you should make sure you stand out.

You should contact the people with a follow-up call one to two days after the appointment. If they told you they needed to talk it over, ask if they have had time to make any decisions. If they are still vague, send them a letter briefly outlining the project you discussed and confirm the price. State in your letter that you would enjoy working with them. Inject a personal note: something that you discussed during the appointment.

There have been many times that I thought I'd lost a bid, only to receive an order from that person a few months later. Some people are planners, they want to get an idea of the cost and then save for it or think about it for a while. In any case, if you use the follow-up methods we've talked about, you will increase your odds of being the person that they call back to do the work. It would be unrealistic to expect to win every bid, but if you portray a professional image, are prepared, and follow up your bids accordingly, you will be one step ahead of the competition.

After the Sale

Now that you've sold the job, there's more work to be done. The first thing you will want to do (especially in the beginning) is have the contractor check your material estimates. If you have sold an upholstery job, have the upholsterer pick up the furniture and double-check your yardage estimate before you order the fabric. If you sold draperies, have your drapery workroom check your yardage by showing them your measurements. The same applies to carpet and wallpaper.

Once you have confirmed the amount of material needed, your next step will be to order it. You can order everything by phone or fax. More and more manufacturers are creating on-line ordering systems on their Web sites as well. Talk to each manufacturer that you deal with to find out if they provide this service. It's easy to get in the habit of ordering by phone because it's faster, but it can create problems. Some of the larger manufacturers will tape-record the conversation so that if there is ever a dispute there will be a record. Even so, your chance of messing up the order is still greater because there are a lot of numbers involved when ordering and mistakes are inevitable. Most of the companies will pro-

Sample Order Form

Quantity	I/S O/S	Width	Length	Controls	Stack	Valance	Style	Color	Price
1	o/s	75	84	left	left	yes	hop	acorn	350

vide you with ordering forms that can be faxed directly to them. This way you will have the order in black and white. Writing the order on the form will also enable you to check the order again before you send it in. The manufacturer will mail or fax you a confirmation of the order a few days later so you can check it once again. Here is a sample order for a vertical blind. (The specific order forms for all products will be explained in chapter 9.)

Filing System for Orders

You will need to have a progress system for ongoing orders so that you can check on them as they progress. You will need to be able to determine if a product that you've ordered is running late or simply hasn't shown up. I have found the easiest system is to again use an expandable file system set up with dates. Mark the tabs as week 1, 2, 3, and 4. When you place an order, you will always be given a projected delivery date. Simply file the order form under the corresponding week. Check the orders weekly and pull the order forms when the products come in, mark them as delivered, and file them in the appropriate client file. If an order is back ordered or delayed for another reason, mark it as such and refile it in the week that it is expected to arrive.

Timelines

I have seen designers get very busy and forget to order one or two items for a job. It would be embarrassing to have to tell a customer that the reason his vertical blind order didn't get installed as scheduled is because you forgot to order it. This potential problem can be avoided by completing a timeline, or product ordered form, for each job you get. Place it in the file folder and keep that file in your in basket on your desk. Follow the rule that the file stays in the basket until all the products have been ordered. If you are doing a drapery job, your form would look something like the sample timeline on the next page.

The Installation

It's crucial that the installation of the product goes well because you won't be paid until everything is perfect. There are a couple of things you can do to ensure that everything runs smoothly.

First, give the installer specific instructions. If the product is window coverings, list each room and the products and sizes that are to be installed in them. If the installer is laying flooring, be sure to specify the room location for each product. It also helps to provide the installer with your diagram showing how you designed the area. There have been cases when an installer assumed that the wood flooring went in the wrong room and installed it. It would also be beneficial to set up a measuring system with your installers. For instance, if you always measure a house from left to right (facing the front of the house), your installer will know that bedroom number 3 means the third bedroom from the left.

Second, make sure the installer knows what to do if anything goes wrong on the job. Most importantly, the installer should keep quiet about the problem. There is nothing worse than an installer who panics on the job and makes the customer lose confidence in you and your work. The other important thing the installer should do is try to fix the problem. A good installer will make a complicated or problem-ridden installation look like a breeze, while a bad installer will stop at the simplest of obstacles and announce that there are problems and the customer should call you to fix them.

Sample Timeline

Date of order:

_____

Customer:

_____

Products sold:

Orders

Product	Date Ordered	Est. Delivery Date
Fabric		
Lining		
Tassels		
Hardware		
Work order to workroom		
Installation scheduled		

To Go or Not to Go

Once your business starts to take off, you will have to make some hard choices regarding your time. In the beginning you will have time to go to most of the installations to check on the progress of the job and collect the balance on the invoice. Once you start to get busier, you will have to spend more time selling. Your absence at the installation can create a problem with some customers, so you will have to learn how to prioritize. For instance, if you've sold a job of custom draperies, it's more important that you be at that job than at a miniblind job. Some of your customers will request that you be there while others won't care as long as the outcome of the job is good. Generally, the more specialized installations require your presence. For instance, if the installation involves a wood floor with an inlaid pattern, you should definitely be at the installation to direct the installer with specific instructions. The same applies to most custom drapery jobs. You are the person who designed the draperies, so you should be at the installation to ensure that they are installed correctly. It's not always necessary that you stay through the entire installation, but at the minimum make an appearance at the larger ones.

If you don't plan on being at an installation, ask your installer to collect the balance due and give the customer a receipt. You will have to provide him or her with the invoice and the paperwork with the measurements on it. Make sure that your customer is aware that it's all right to give the installer the balance.

Managing Your Sales

It's easy to become overwhelmed in the home-based interior design business because not only will you be responsible for achieving your self-imposed sales quotas, but you will also be responsible for the installations and all the little details that lead up to it. It's wise to start by setting small, attainable goals in the beginning. Then take those goals and create a plan that will allow you to accomplish them. If your goal is to have three appointments per day, and each appointment lasts approximately two hours, that's six selling hours a day. Add in time for the bookkeeping (one hour) and time for figuring bids and ordering products (three hours), and you must plan on working ten hours per day to meet your goal. If that's too much, cut down to two appointments per day and plan on marketing higher-end neighborhoods so each sale will bring in more income. Your goals will change over time as you become more confident. You will also start to establish a selling pattern. If you know that your average sale is $2,000, you will have no problem setting your sales goals.

Next you will need to work on your time management. I've found that lists are imperative in this business. I usually will end my day by making a list of the things I didn't get to that day and leaving it on my desk. I'll start the next day by finishing that list before I do anything else. Set your appointments so that you have either the morning or the afternoon open to take care of paperwork.

Be sure not to set your appointments too close together or you'll spend your time apologizing for arriving late. Allow enough time to cover measuring, choosing fabrics and materials, bid work, and some small talk. An hour is usually enough time for not-so-difficult jobs, such as flooring, hard window coverings (miniblinds, verticals, etc.), and upholstery. Allow one and one-half to two hours for more complicated jobs such as draperies and wallpaper. On these types of appointments, the customer will want enough time to look at all of the choices you have brought along.

Another way you can make the best use of your time is to organize your price sheets and formula guides into a sales manual. I will help you put together yours in the next chapter.

Chapter Nine

Product Overview

This is it: the chapter you've been waiting for. You now have enough basic knowledge of the design business and how it works to start studying the specifics of the products that you will sell. Remember, it's important always to present yourself as a professional, and professionals know their products. Over time you will gain more and more knowledge of the products as you work with them, but in the meantime you must be as well equipped as possible.

I have designed this chapter in a way that is most conducive to learning. It's important to know the basics of the products, but it's not necessary to memorize each of the many formulas and charts. It is, however, important to know where to look for the information. We will put together your sales manual in this chapter, and that will serve as a reference guide for when you are on appointments. You will know exactly where to look for price guides, yardage formulas, and your selling price point guidelines.

Each product topic is subdivided into sections in this chapter: hard-line window coverings, soft treatment window coverings, bedding and accessories, flooring, wallpaper, and upholstery. I will discuss the measuring guidelines for each product. I will also provide formulas and charts that will help you determine how much product it will take to do the job. I have also included relevant term glossaries and manufacturer source lists for each of the products. A section on putting together your sales manual will help you determine which of these materials to include. There are sample price lists and practice problems at the end of the chapter that will allow you to practice pricing each of the products before you actually go on an appointment. Take the time to work the problems because doing so will help you feel more confident.

Section One: Hard-Line Window Coverings

This section will cover all hard-line window coverings: miniblinds, vertical blinds, shades, and shutters. The term *hard-line* refers to window coverings that are hard or durable in nature, unlike soft window treatments such as draperies and valances. We will start this section with a glossary so that when we discuss the specifics we will be using the same language.

Hard-Lines Glossary

CELLULAR SHADE. A second generation of pleated shades. Fabric is double layered and shaped like a honeycomb. Cord system operates the same as for a regular pleated shade except that the cord runs through the middle of the honeycomb, which eliminates light holes. Great for energy efficiency, and fabric is luxurious. They will fit into any window application: inside or outside mounts, arches, circles, skylights, etc. Cost runs approximately twice the price of a miniblind. Available in hundreds of colors, and they range from transparent to opaque; usually white on the side facing the street.

MINIBLIND. A blind that has metal slats running horizontally. Available in ½-inch, 1-inch, or 2-inch slats. Will work in most window situations, although they can become costly in odd-shaped windows. Slats can be adjusted for light control or blind can be pulled up and down. Usually comes with a two-slat valance. One of the least expensive products on a standard-shaped window. Available in hundreds of colors.

PLEATED SHADE. Shade consists of a single layer of fabric that is uniformly pleated. Cord system operates the same as a miniblind, so light holes are visible. Shade can be pulled up and down only; there are no slats to adjust like a miniblind. Cost is between a miniblind and a cellular shade. Will fit most odd-shaped windows. Available in many colors, and fabrics range from transparent to opaque (although the opaque will still have light holes).

SHUTTERS. Available in 2-, 2½-, 3½-, and 4½-inch slats. Usually made from solid wood and painted or stained. Recent variations include vinyl shutters. Operates as a panel

Measuring for Hard-Line Products

Unfortunately, most of the hard-line products are measured differently. They will all be measured to fit either inside the window or outside. This measurement is referred to as an inside mount or outside mount. An *inside mount* is when the product is installed inside the window frame; with an *outside mount* the product is mounted directly onto the wall. With

with adjustable slats. Can be customized to fit any window or style, depending on the size slat and the number of desired panels. One of the most expensive products. Available in twenty to thirty preselected colors, but most manufacturers will work with a customer's custom color for an additional charge.

SILHOUETTES. One of the most innovative products on the market today; constructed of sheer fabric slats. Operates on a continuous cord loop, and the entire shade rolls up into the headrail. Available in horizontal style (silhouettes) or vertical style (vynettes). Available in approximately fifty colors. Semiprivate when closed, transparent when open. Very expensive; the price compares to wood shutters.

WOOD BLIND. Operates and looks like a miniblind except that the slats are made of wood instead of aluminum. Available in 1-, 2-, and 3-inch slats. Paint, stain, or faux finishes are available. Approximately half the cost of shutters.

VERTICAL BLIND. A vertical running vane that is attached to a headrail. The vanes are constructed of aluminum, PVC, or fabric. The fabric vanes come freehanging or are inserted into a PVC backing. Available in 2-inch or 3½-inch vanes. Vanes can rotate 180 degrees or be pulled across track to open or close. Great solution for sliding glass doors. Available in hundreds of colors. Depending on the vertical selected, cost can run a little more than a miniblind or as much as a shutter. (Each pattern and style are priced individually.)

WOVEN WOODS. Shades, made from natural fibers such as bamboo, rattan, or jute, which roll up or hang in roman shade style. Moderately priced.

an inside mount the manufacturer will take the necessary deductions to ensure a proper fit, while an outside mount will be manufactured to your exact specifications.

You will have to pay attention to the window structure and what is around it. If the molding wraps inside the window, it would be impossible to install a miniblind as an inside mount because the molding would interfere with the operation of the blind. On the other hand, if the customer has stenciled around the outside of the window, you would want to fit the product on the inside so the stenciling wouldn't be covered up. Pay attention to the wall space around the window as well as the architecture itself. If the window has furniture or some other obstacle sitting right next to it, you won't be able to utilize that space for an outside mount.

Another obstacle to watch for is the way the window opens. In some houses the window may open with a crank, and that would make it impossible to fit a product inside the window because the crank would interfere with the operation of the blind. Some windows may have only a half-inch area around the inside frame, and that isn't enough room for some brackets. Most of the time you will have to use common sense.

On all the price lists you get from the manufacturers, there will be specifications of the products. It is imperative to know how each product is constructed because that information will come into play when you are considering the installation.

You should always use a good 1-inch steel tape measure. There will be times when you measure large windows, and anything less will not stand up. An inadequate tape measure will make measuring both awkward and inaccurate. Another rule for measuring is *never* to use a cloth measuring tape. You must measure to the nearest ⅛ inch for these products, and a cloth tape won't even come close.

There will be times when you are on an appointment and the client will tell you that all the windows are the same size so you only need to measure one of them. While the windows may be approximately the same size, it's doubtful that they are so exact. Remember, you are measuring to the eighth of an inch. For instance, let's imagine that one window measured was 35⅜ inches and the others looked the same so you ordered all the blinds that size. When the installer tried to hang them, one of the windows measured 35⅛ inches, and the blind would not fit that window because it was ⅜ (or ¼) inch too big.

You have more leeway on outside mounts because they are installed directly onto the wall, but you still need to pay attention to the areas around the window. Make sure you have enough room for the brackets. There will be other obstacles, such as butting walls and low ceilings. It would be impossible to cover everything you will come up against because every house is built differently. Most of your price lists will give you specific measuring instructions for problem windows. Again, common sense will be your best-used tool when measuring. On the following pages there are measuring charts that will give you the general rules for measuring each product.

Measurement Instructions

Miniblinds/Wood Blinds
(Inside Mount)

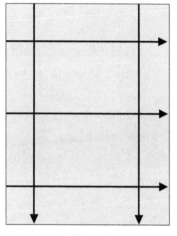

Width
Measure the width in three different locations (see fig. 1). Use shortest measurement.

Length
Measure the length in two different locations (see fig. 1). Use longest measurement.

(Fig. 1)

Miniblinds/Wood Blinds
(Outside Mount)

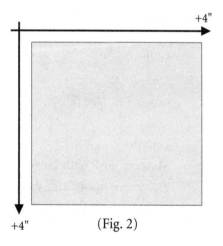

+4"

Width
Measure the exact width that you want covered. Add 4" (see fig. 2).

Length
Measure the exact length that you want covered. Add 4" (see fig. 2).

+4"   (Fig. 2)

Miniblinds on French Doors

Width
Measure the glass width to cover molding (watch for door knobs) (see fig. 3).

Length
Measure the glass length. Add 4" (see fig. 3).

Standard measurement for French Doors is 24" x 68".

When ordering, specify hold downs and spacers.

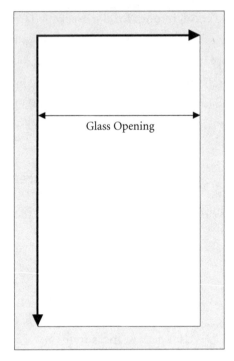

(Fig. 3)

Vertical Blinds
(Inside Mount)

Width
Measure the width along top of window (see fig. 4).

Length
Measure the length in two places (see fig. 4). Use shortest measurement. (see Fig. 4).

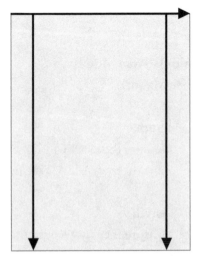

(Fig. 4)

Vertical Blinds
(Outside Mount)

Width
Measure the exact width that you want covered. Add 4" (see fig. 5).

Length
Measure the exact length that you want covered. Add 4" (see fig. 5).

+4"

+4"   (Fig. 5)

Pleated Shades/Cellular Shades
(Inside Mount)

Width
Measure the width in three different locations (See fig. 6). Use shortest measurement.

Length
Measure the length in two different locations (see fig. 6). Use longest measurement.

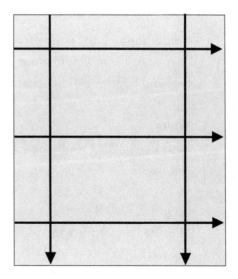

(Fig. 6)

Arch Window
(Perfect Arches)

Width
Measure the exact width
(see fig. 7).

Length
Measure the exact center length.
Length measurement should
be exactly half the width for a
perfect arch (see fig. 7).

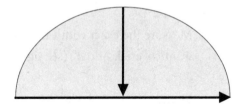

(Fig. 7)

Arch Window
(Nonperfect Arches)

Note: If the arch is a nonperfect arch,
use an outside mount to avoid light
gaps and bunching of material.

Width
Measure the exact width. Add 2"
(see fig. 8).

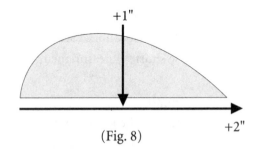

+1"

(Fig. 8)

+2"

Length
Measure the exact length. Add 1"
(see fig. 8).

Silhouettes

Note: Product cannot be cut down. The measurements must be perfect.

Width
Measure the width in three different locations (see fig. 9).
Use shortest measurement.

Length
Measure the length in two different locations (see fig. 9).
Use shortest measurement.

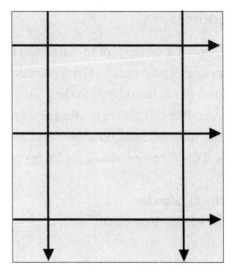

(Fig. 9)

All Products

When you are covering just the square part of an irregularly shaped window, measure as you would for an inside mount.

When ordering: Order an inside mount with outside mount brackets.

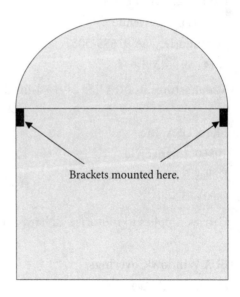

Brackets mounted here.

Sources

There are thousands of manufacturers in business and it would be impossible for me to list them all. I have tried to include a selection that varies in products and prices in each of the subsections. In addition to these lists, you must do research on your own by reading trade magazines and talking to other people in the interior design business. It may take you a few tries to find the manufacturer that best fits your needs. That's okay; keep trying until you find the right one. Here's the list for hard-line window coverings.

The Blindmaker
2013 Centimeter Circle
Austin, TX 78758
(800) 999–5444

Manufactures Graber products, which include all hard-lines and drapery hardware.

DelMar Window Coverings
c/o Levolor Home Fashions
7400 Hazard Avenue
Westminster, CA 92683-5031
(714) 891–4311

Manufactures its own line of hard-lines, including woven woods.

Elero, USA, Inc.
10860 Adler Circle
Dallas, TX 75238-1347
(800) 752–8677

Carries supplies to motorize all hard-lines and soft treatments.

FUA Window Coverings
899 S. Castell Avenue
New Braunfels, TX 78130
(888) 857–9195

Manufactures an exquisite line of handwoven woven woods.

Hunter Douglas

P.O. Box 2

Frostburg, MO 21532-9985

(800) 365–3399

Manufactures its own line of hard-lines.

Kirsch Corporation

309 N. Prospect Street

Sturgis, MI 49091-1598

(616) 659–5100

Manufactures most hard-lines and drapery hardware.

Lafayette Venetian Blinds

P.O. Box 2838

West Lafayette, IN 45906–0838

(800) 342–5523

Fabricates all major brands of hard-lines as well as fabrics and wallpaper. Also fabricates draperies, bedding, and accessories.

Levolor/Kirsch Home Fashions Corporation

4110 Premier Drive

High Point, NC 27265-8145

(336) 812–8181

Manufactures its own line of hard-lines.

Nanik

P.O. Box 1766

Wausau, WI 54402-1766

(800) 422–4544

Manufactures wood blinds and shutters. Also manufactures a unique product called Optix.

O'Hair Shutters

P.O. Box 2764

Lubbock, TX 79048

(800) 582–2625

Manufactures shutters.

Timber Blind and Shutter

800 E. Elm Street

McKinney, TX 75069

(877) 434-2000

Manufactures wood blinds and fabricate woven woods, cellular shades, shutters, and miniblinds.

Vinylbilt Shutters

861 Roundtree Dairy Road

Woodbridge, Ontario L415W3

Canada

(800) 222–7934

Manufactures vinyl interior shutters.

Section Two: Soft Window Treatments

The term *soft treatment* refers to draperies, valances, cornices, custom bedding, table rounds, and pillows. Basically, a soft treatment is any product that makes use of fabric. Your drapery workroom will fabricate all these products. You will need to be able to give a bid on these products, and in order to do that you must have the formulas and charts that I have included in this section. Even the most experienced designers usually have their workroom double-check the yardage requirement before actually placing the order. The drapery workrooms make the product, so it's possible that they may be able to save you from a mistake early on. For estimating purposes, you will need to be able to figure labor and fabric for soft treatment products. Let's start again with a glossary of terms relevant to soft treatments.

Soft Treatment Glossary

CASCADE. A piece of fabric that hangs in a zigzag line down the side or sides of a drapery treatment. It is sometimes double sided with a contrast fabric.

CENTER DRAW. A pair of draperies that open and close from the middle.

CORNICE. A wooden boxlike structure covered with foam and then fabric. The edge can be straight, scalloped, or made to any shape you want.

CUSTOM-MADE DRAPERIES. Draperies made to individual specifications to fit a window.

CUT LENGTH. The length of the fabric after allowances have been made for the heading and the hem.

FINIALS. Decorative pieces on the end of a drapery rod such as balls or leaf-shaped designs.

FINISHED LENGTH. The actual length that the draperies will be when completed.

FULLNESS. A measurement of the drapery or valance that takes into account any necessary bunching. If a drapery is 250 percent or 2.5x full, there are 2.5 inches of fabric for every 1 inch of rod. Most custom draperies are 2.5x full, with a few exceptions. Most sheers are 3x full to increase privacy. Heavier fabrics are sometimes made at 2x fullness because they are so bulky. Flat valances are 1x full because they are not gathered.

JABOT. A cascadelike treatment that is used in the middle of swag treatments. It is usually one-half the length of cascades.

LINING. The backing used for a drapery. Most custom drapes are lined.

ONE-WAY DRAW. A drapery that opens and closes from only one side. Most often used on a sliding glass door.

OVERLAP. The part of the center-draw drapery that is closest to the middle. It is what makes the pair overlap to avoid light gaps. It's usually 3½ inches on each side.

PANEL. One half of a pair of draperies. Used for one-way draws.

PATTERN REPEAT. Drapery fabrics that have patterns have pattern repeats. The distance (in inches) between the start of a pattern to where it begins again is the measurement of the repeat.

PINCH-PLEAT DRAPERIES. Draperies that are attached to traverse rods.

RETURN. The distance between the face of a drapery and the wall. The average return for a drapery treatment is 3½ inches. Add 2 inches more for every overtreatment you add. For instance, if you are measuring for sheers, draperies, and a valance, plan for a 3½-inch return for the sheers, a 5½-inch return for the draperies, and a 7½-inch return for the valance. This return allows room for the undertreatments to move without getting caught in one another.

ROD POCKET. A hollow sleeve in the drapery or valance where the rod is to slide through.

SHIRRED DRAPERY. A drapery or valance in which the fabric is gathered along the rod.

SWAG. A valance in which the fabric is draped over a rod or attached to a board. The effect is a graceful flow of fabric. Used in conjunction with cascades and jabots.

TIEBACKS. Decorative hardware or pieces of fabric used to hold the drapery in place.

TRAVERSE ROD. A metal drapery rod with a pulley mechanism for drawing curtains.

VALANCE. A horizontal fabric treatment to be used with or without draperies.

WIDTH. A width of fabric is exactly that: one width of fabric (the actual width in inches varies). It is also a term used by drapery workrooms to arrive at their charges. When calculating a drapery cost, you will break it down into widths and yards. Use the width figure to determine the workroom cost and the yardage figure to determine the fabric cost.

Measuring and Calculating Yardage for Soft Treatments

The majority of the soft treatments you design will be mounted on the outside of the window. When you calculate a drapery, simply measure the window opening and it will be up to you to determine how much wider and taller you want the draperies to be. You should figure a minimum of 6 inches on each side to eliminate any light gap (4 if it's really tight), and 4 to 6 inches above the window to accommodate the drapery hardware. Other than that, there are no rules. Some customers may want to cover a window along with the entire wall to give the illusion of a wall-to-wall window; others may want to start the drapery just below the ceiling to add height to a room. Some customers will be on a budget, and you will be able to cut costs by just covering the area needed (the window) and adding the minimum number of inches.

Measuring for a valance is just as easy. You should measure the width of the window opening and add 4 to 6 inches. The length will depend on the type of valance you are creating. Most valances range from 12 to 36 inches. If you are covering a small window, the valance should be on the shorter side, but if you are working with a large window you are free to use a longer valance. You will need to eye the window with your tape measure and get your customer's opinion in order to determine the actual length of the treatment.

If you are in doubt about the way your design will look on the window, you can draw it to scale on your graph paper, which will also help your client visualize your design. You can make it come to life by using colored pencils that coordinate with the fabric colors the client has selected. If you have a client who doesn't seem to understand your design but expresses trust in you, you may want to consider drawing the design for the client anyway. It's amazing how two people can be talking about the same drapery but visualizing two entirely different treatments. On the next few pages there are formulas and charts to help you figure drapery, valance, bedding, tablecloth, and pillow bids. Be sure to use them for bidding, but take your measurements to your workroom and have them check your yardage before actually placing the order (especially on the first few jobs).

Pinch-Pleat or Shirred Draperies

To determine the number of widths:

> Finished width + 12" (for hems) + return size = A
>
> A x 2.5 (or desired fullness) = B
>
> B ÷ 48 = number of widths (round up to the next even number)

To determine the number of yards needed:

> Finished length + 20" x number of widths = C
>
> C ÷ 36 = number of yards

Now that you have the number of widths and yards, you need to determine the type of drapery hardware that you need. Your manufacturer will provide you with a catalog that shows the different types of drapery hardware and its varied uses. You will also find the price for the hardware in the catalog. You will need the

Checklist of Charges for Pinch-Pleat or Shirred Draperies

Number of widths x price per width
Number of yards x price of fabric
Number of yards x price of lining
Price of drapery hardware
Installation charge

same amount of lining as fabric. The last thing you will need to add to your bid is the installation charge. (That will be in your installer's price list.)

Tieback Yardage

A drapery can be held back with decorative tieback holders (they can be ordered through your drapery hardware source) or fabric ties. You can use the same fabric as the drapery or use a contrast fabric to add interest. A tieback is usually 18 inches per width of fabric. Your workroom will charge you a price per pair and your installer will also have a tieback installation charge. Add these charges together with the fabric requirements to arrive at your cost.

1 width	18" long
1½ widths	27" long
2 widths	36" long
2½ widths	45" long
3 widths	54" long

Figuring Swag Yardage and Labor

Swags can be draped over a rod or mounted on a board. Check with your local workroom for prices. The charges are usually figured per linear foot. You should line all swags because it will make them drape more easily. Add the price of the fabric, the price of the lining, the workroom labor charge, and the installation charge to determine your price. Add your markup to arrive at the retail price. You should never use a heavy fabric because the swags will look stiff and not flow as they should. Here is a guideline for the number of swags needed, determined by the width of the window and the yardage required to make them.

Swag Guideline and Yardage Chart

Face Width	up to 40"	41–70"	71–100"	101–120"	121–140"
Number of swags	1	1–2	3	3–4	4–5
Yardage	2	5	9½	9½	11½

Figuring Cascade Yardage

A cascade is a piece of fabric that falls at both ends of a swag. It can be self-lined, or a contrast fabric can be used. If you are self-lining the cascade, double the yardage on the following chart. If you are using a contrast lining, order the same amount as the face yardage. Your workroom will charge you per pair of cascades.

Cascade Yardage Chart

Length	up to 36"	37–48"	49–50"	61–81"	85–96"
Face width	1½	1½	2	2½	3

Figuring Rod Pocket Valances

Rod pocket valances are *shirred* (gathered) onto a rod. You can shirr the fabric onto the rod by itself or you can use a rod pocket as a header for a free-falling valance. Here are the formulas you need to determine the amount of widths and yardage that you will require. Again, you will need to add the cost of the fabric, lining, workroom labor, drapery hardware, and installation to determine your cost.

To determine the number of widths

Rod width ÷ width of fabric = number of widths (round up to next even number)

To determine the number of yards

Finished length + [2 x (heading size + pocket size)] + 20" = length of cuts
Number of widths x length of cuts ÷ 36 = number of yards needed

Note: Add one pattern repeat per cut length for print fabrics.

Cornice Boards

A cornice board is a decorative piece of wood that is covered with foam and fabric. It is a perfect way to add the softness of fabric into a room that utilizes straight lines. A cornice board will look great in offices or contemporary homes where flowery draperies won't work. All cornices should be lined. Your workroom will charge a fee per linear foot. You won't need drapery hardware for cornice boards because the boards are mounted directly onto the wall. Add the cost of the fabric, lining, workroom charges, and installation to arrive at your cost.

Yardage for Solid-Color Cornices

Cornice face width + 2 returns + 8" (standard allowance) x 2.5
(if fabric is not flat) = total number of inches
Total number of inches ÷ 36 = amount of yardage needed (round up)

Yardage for Print Cornices

Cornice length + 2 returns + 6" (standard allowance) = cut length
Cornice width + 2 returns + 8" (standard allowance) x 2.5
(if fabric is not flat) = Total width ÷ fabric width + number of cuts
(round up to next nearest number)
Number of cuts x cut length ÷ 36" = required yardage (round up)

Upholstery

Upholstery work is a natural way to increase your sales volume. When you are designing the draperies and wallpaper in a room, it stands to reason that the furniture will need a new look too. You can give bids based on the chart I have provided, but once again it's a good idea to utilize your upholsterer and ask him or her to verify your yardage after the furniture has been picked up. You can adjust your client's bill afterward if you have misjudged the amount of fabric needed.

When giving an upholstery bid, you will first need to help your client select the fabric and then use the chart to determine the number of yards needed. Your upholsterer will have given you a chart with his or her labor charges. Add the cost of the fabric, labor charge, and any delivery charge and then calculate your markup.

After you have a signed contract and a deposit, schedule a time for your upholsterer to pick up the furniture. Once the upholsterer has done that, he or she should call you with the yardage requirement. Then you can order the fabric. When the furniture is complete, you will need to schedule another appointment for the upholsterer to drop off the furniture. You can either ask the upholsterer to pick up the balance or go to the appointment and collect it yourself.

In addition to using this information, you will have to do much research on your own. These charts and formulas are meant to be only a guide to ease the process of bidding. I highly recommend that you take a class or work for a competitor before attempting to give a bid. If you can't, be sure to let your workroom help you with the process. Draperies are a fun and challenging aspect of the design business. You can

Upholstery Chart

Furniture	Yardage Needed
Sofa under 72" long	14 yards
Sofa over 72" long	15 yards
Sofa over 84" long	16 yards
Lounge chair	7–8 yards
Wing chair	7–8 yards
Recliner	7–8 yards
Barrel chair	7 yards
Dining room chair (seat only)	1–2 yards
Dining room chair (seat and back)	2–3 yards
Small bench	3–4 yards
Medium bench	4 yards
Large bench or ottoman	4–6 yards
Twin headboard	3 yards
Full headboard	3½ yards
Queen headboard	4 yards
King headboard	5 yards
California (CA) king headboard	6 yards

make a room look dramatic with a unique, bold drapery on the window, or you can make a room look cozy and inviting with different choices of textures and styles.

Section Three: Bedding and Accessories

Measuring

Adding custom bedding, pillows, and table rounds to an order can be quite profitable. It will add a custom look to a bedroom that is impossible to achieve with off-the-rack products. Your local workroom will include the price of these products on its price list. I have listed the standard sizes of mattresses in this section to help you with the bedding measurements. The measurements reflect width times length times drop (to top of box spring). Keep in mind that you should ask customers to make the bed exactly like they will when they use the new bedspread or comforter. A thick blanket could make a lot of difference on how the bedding will fall, so be sure always to measure. When measuring for a bedspread or comforter, you must get the following measurements:

Measurement Requirements for Bedding

1. Width of mattress
2. Length of mattress
3. Drop from top of mattress to floor (use this if you are measuring for a bedspread)
4. Drop from top of mattress to desired length (use this if you are measuring for a coverlet or comforter, not a bedspread)
5. Drop from top of box spring to floor (use this measurement for the dust ruffle)

Yardage for Bedspreads

The following is the amount of fabric you will need for a standard throw bedspread. The yardage is based on solid fabrics. For print fabrics, add two pattern repeats. There are many different styles of bedding, and they all have different yardage requirements. Be sure to ask your workroom for guidelines.

A dust ruffle, shams, throw pillows, and table rounds are also an easy add-on to your sale. The price of all these products can be figured quickly and easily. Following are some simple calculations for figuring yardage for these products. Again, check with your local workroom for labor costs.

Bedspread Yardage Requirements	
Size	**48" or 54" fabric**
Twin	8 yards
Full	8 yards
Queen	12 yards
King	12 yards
CA King	12 yards

Standard Mattress Sizes	
Twin	39 x 75 x 21
Full	54 x 75 x 21
Queen	60 x 80 x 21
King	72 x 84 x 21
CA king	78 x 80 x 21

Gathered-Style Dust Ruffle Yardage

The yardage requirements listed here are based on solid fabric that is gathered at 2.5x fullness.

Dust Ruffle Yardage Requirements	
Size	**Yardage**
Twin	7½ yards
Full	8 yards
Queen	10 yards
King	11 yards
CA king	11 yards

Yardage for Pillow Shams

Yardage needed for flanged and corded shams is 2 yards. If you want a ruffle, add 1 yard for each ruffle. These yardage requirements are for shams measuring up to 36 by 21 inches. Again, there are many variations of pillow shams, so you will need to ask your workroom for specific quotes.

Yardage for Throw Pillows

Round or square knife-edged 14-inch pillows require ½ yard each. Add 1½ yards for each self-lined ruffle. Ask your workroom for labor and pillow insert prices.

Yardage for Table Covers

For a round tablecloth up to 90 inches in diameter, you will need 5½ yards. For a rectangular tablecloth up to 60 by 102 inches, you will need 6 yards. Add 2 yards if there is a ruffle.

Sources

Here's a list of selected manufacturers of drapery and upholstery fabric, bedding, and related accessories.

Ado
P.O. Box 3447
Spartanburg, SC 29304-3447
(800) 845–0918
Carries an extensive line of seamless sheers, laces, jacquards, prints, and embroideries.

✓ **Fabricut Fabrics**
9303 E. Forty-sixth Street
Tulsa, OK 74145-4595
(800) 999–8200
Carries drapery and upholstery fabrics. Also fabricates draperies, bedding, and accessories.

Kasmir Fabrics
2229 Monitor
Dallas, TX 75207
(800) 527–4630
Carries drapery and upholstery fabrics. Also fabricates draperies, bedding, and accessories.

Lady Ann Fabrics
801 Pasadena Avenue South
St. Petersburg, FL 33707-2033
(727) 344–1819
Carries drapery fabrics and drapery hardware.

✓ **Robert Allen**
50 Peachview Boulevard
Gaffney, SC 29341
(864) 489–6667
Manufactures drapery and upholstery fabrics. Also has an extensive line of trim and tassels.

Scroll Fabrics
4500 Highlands Parkwa, SE
Smyrna, GA 30082-5187
(770) 432–7228
Manufactures all custom bedding and accessories.

Schumacher Waverly
P.O. Box 6002
Newark, DE 19714
(302) 454–3200
Manufactures drapery and upholstery fabrics. Also fabricates draperies and bedding. Carries a line of coordinating wallpaper.

Van Lathem
105 W. Corriher Avenue
Salisbury, NC 28144
(704) 642–1623
An outstanding collection of fabrics and trims.

Section Four: Flooring

Among the types of flooring you will have to offer are carpet, wood, tile, and vinyl. As I stated earlier, most of your flooring jobs will come from clients for whom you are already designing their home. Because flooring manufacturers give special pricing to large carpet stores that do a lot of business, it will be nearly impossible for you to be competitive with them. In the instances when the client is looking for carpet and shopping around for the best price, you probably won't get the job. But, if you are working with a client and putting together a complete design package, the client won't be concerned with the price of the flooring because you will have quoted one price for the entire job.

You should know the basics of flooring so you will appear knowledgeable on your appointments, but it's not necessary for you to be able to bid a job to the exact yard (unless you want to open a carpet store, in which case you are reading the wrong book). In the earlier discussion about contractors in chapter 7, I told you to make sure your installer would measure your jobs and give you a yardage count. You will have the basic formula to give an estimate for carpet, and if the customer wants to proceed, you should have your installer measure the house and give you the exact yardage needed. From there you can adjust your bid appropriately and order the goods. I have always explained to my customers that the installer can measure and arrive at the smallest amount of yardage needed because the installer knows where to seam it. Once I have the exact yardage needed, I will either reduce or increase the bill depending on how I estimated the job. We will start this section with a glossary of terms for flooring as we did in the previous sections.

Flooring Glossary

BERBER. A Berber is a style of carpet that is not cut on top. The yarn forms little continuous loops. Available in solid colors or speckled patterns. Feels harder underfoot than thick plush carpets but wears better. Good for informal settings.

CUT BERBER. A softer Berber. Instead of loops, the yarn is cut. Wears almost as well as a Berber while still giving the look of casualness.

CUT-LOOP. A style of carpet that is mixed, with both small loops and cut yarn. Also known as sculptured carpet. Available in a variety of colors.

(flooring glossary, *continued*)

FRIEZE. The yarn on this type of carpet is twisted very tight, giving the appearance of a two-toned surface. This carpet is good for high-traffic areas because it won't show wear and you will not be able to see most footprints.

GROUT. A substance that is installed between tile squares. Available in many colors. The same color as the tile will give a smooth appearance, and a contrast color will give the area interest.

PAD. A urethane cushion that is installed under carpet. It makes the carpet softer to walk on and keeps the carpet looking new for longer. Some carpets, such as Berber, have specific requirements for the type of pad to use with them in order to get the warranties. Ask your manufacturers for their requirements.

PLUSH. A carpet with a cut pile that is very rich in appearance. It is also called a velvet. The appearance is deceiving in this carpet because the yarn is not as dense as a Saxony and will not wear as well.

SAXONY. Like plush, this carpet also has a cut pile, but it is shorter. The yarns are packed closer together, which gives it greater wearability.

TILE. Ceramic tile squares that can be laid on the floor, walls, or countertops. Sizes range from 4 to 15 inches. Available in hundreds of colors and textures.

WOOD FLOORING. Available in planks or laminate and in many stains and grains.

Measuring for an Estimate

Following is a formula for square yardage to use when you are giving an estimate for all flooring except tile (which is figured by the square foot and has its own formula). You will also need to include padding (the same yardage as your carpet), installation (also figured by the yard), and any freight fee that the carpet manufacturer charges.

Figuring Square Yards for Carpet, Wood Floors, and Vinyl

1. Measure the width and length of each room to be covered. (Include closets and room cutouts but measure them as separate rooms.)
2. If you measured them in inches, convert to feet.
3. Multiply the width by the length and divide by 9.
4. Round up to the next nearest number. This is your square yardage estimate.

Figuring Square Feet for Tile

1. Measure the width and length of each room to be covered. (Include closets and room cutouts but measure them as separate rooms.)
2. If you measured in inches, convert to feet.
3. Multiply width by length.
4. Round up to the next nearest number. This is your square footage estimate.

Sources

Anderson Hardwood Floors
P.O. Box 1155
Old Laurens Road
Clinton, SC 29325
(864) 833–6250
Manufactures hardwood floors.

Armstrong World Industries
313 W. Liberty Street
Lancaster, PA 17603-2717
(717) 397–0611
Manufactures vinyl flooring.

Emser International
8431 Santa Monica Boulevard
Los Angeles, CA 90069-4294
(323) 650–2000
Manufactures ceramic tile.

Interceramic, Inc.
2333 S. Jupiter Road
Garland, TX 75041
(214) 503–5500
Manufactures ceramic tile.

L. D. Brinkman & Corporation
4267 Dividend
San Antonio, TX 78219-2699
(210) 337–6990
Distributes all major brands of carpet, tile, wood floors, and vinyl flooring. It is a nationwide company with distributors in most major cities.

Mohawk
P.O. Box 12069
Calhoun, GA 30703
(706) 629–7721
Manufactures carpet.

Shaw Carpets
P.O. Box 15671
Dalton, GA 30722-1527
(800) 241–4031
Manufactures carpet.

Stanton Royal Dutch Carpet
207 Robbins Lane
Syosset, NY 11791
(800) 729–2946
Distributes carpet.

S & S Mills Direct
P.O. Box 1568
Dalton, GA 30722
(800) 241–4013
Manufactures carpet.

Unique Carpets, Ltd.
2050 Carlos Avenue
Ontario, CA 91761
(800) 826–5520
Manufactures carpet. Large selection of wool and sisal carpets.

Section Five: Wallpaper

Selling and measuring for wallpaper is surprisingly easy. The hardest part of it is steering your customer toward a selection because there are so many patterns and styles to choose from. Before you go to your appointment, try to narrow down the style and colors that the customer is interested in. Try to take as few books to the appointment as you can (while still maintaining a good selection). Your job will be to help the client choose the wallpaper. After your client has made the selection, measure the room to determine how many rolls you will need. Have your wallpaper contractor measure the room before you order it, just as you would for carpet. Some of the patterns are hard to match, and certain architectural aspects of a room may make a difference in the amount you need. The chart in this section gives general estimates.

Most of the wallpaper companies will require that you order the wallpaper in double rolls: that is, two rolls at once. Some manufacturers will allow you to return unused rolls for a nominal fee, but check with your manufacturer to determine their policy. Make sure that you determine whether the wallpaper is sold in double or single rolls because that will affect your price. (Some manufacturers list the wallpaper at single-roll prices but insist that you buy it in double rolls.)

A recent problem has changed the way wallpaper manufacturers price their product. The emergence of the toll-free (800 or 888 area code) numbers in the back of magazines has made it harder for retailers to stay competitive. Some consumers will go into a retail store and write down the item numbers of the wallpaper they are interested in. Then they will call the toll-free number listed in the back of a magazine and order the product at a sub-stantially reduced price. To combat this problem, some manufacturers have scrambled the item numbers that are attached to the patterns and then give the retailers a key for order-ing purposes. When the customer tries to call in the false item numbers, there is no match.

Sources

Blonder Wallcoverings
3950 Prospect Avenue
Cleveland, OH 44115–2795
(800) 321–4070
Carries wallpaper, borders, and coordi-nating fabrics.

Brewster Wallcoverings
67 Pacella Park Drive
Randolph, MA 02368-1776
(800) 366–1701
Carries wallpaper, borders, and coordi-nating fabrics. Also offers coordinating accessories, including bedspreads, valances, dust ruffles, and pillows.

Hunter & Co.
1945 W. Green Drive
High Point, NC 27261-2363
(800) 523–8387
Carries wallpaper and accessories.

Olney Wallcoverings
P.O. Box 1172
Spartanburg, SC 29304
(864) 585–2431
Carries wallpaper, borders, and coordi-nating fabrics.

Wallpaper Chart

Size of Room*	Ceiling Height (in feet)			
	8	9	10	11
8 x 10	10	12	12	14
10 x 10	12	12	14	16
10 x 12	12	14	16	16
10 x 14	14	14	16	16
12 x 12	14	14	16	18
12 x 14	14	16	18	20
12 x 16	16	18	20	20
12 x 18	16	18	20	22
12 x 20	18	20	22	24
14 x 14	16	18	20	22
14 x 16	16	18	20	22
14 x 18	18	20	22	24
14 x 20	18	20	24	26
14 x 22	20	22	24	26
16 x 16	18	20	22	24
16 x 18	18	20	24	26
16 x 20	20	22	24	26
16 x 22	20	24	26	28
16 x 24	22	24	28	30
18 x 18	20	22	24	26
18 x 20	20	24	26	28
18 x 22	22	24	28	30
18 x 24	22	26	28	32

* When ordering a border to coordinate with the wallpaper, simply measure the length of the wall you are planning to cover and convert to feet. Most of the borders come in 15-foot rolls, so you will need to order one border roll per 15 linear feet of wall.

Section Six: Miscellaneous Products

You never know what you will run up against when planning the design of a home. Let's imagine that you are upholstering some kitchen chairs for a client who has five children. In that case, you may want to suggest that you laminate the fabric to protect it against spills and stains. Or you may have a client who wants you to coordinate artwork with the new design of a room. Where do you look for such items? Here's a list of miscellaneous sources for those unusual, hard-to-find products.

Conso
Call (800) 845–2431 for a distributor near you.
Manufactures an extensive line of trims and tassels.

IPA/Southern Laminating, Inc.
6018 Fifth Street
Easley, SC 29640-3407
(864) 859–9000
Carries various laminated fabrics. Also laminates customers' fabrics.

Mastervisions for Windows by Visionary Concepts, Inc.
122 Watch Hill Road
Branford, CT 06405
(203) 483–1641
Manufactures a unique overlay system of window treatment illustrations.

Minutes Matter Systems
796 New Shackle Island Road
Hendersonville, TN 37075
(615) 824–1954
Provides custom forms to help a designer measure a job, work up a bid, or create work orders.

Soft Tex Manufacturing
100 N. Mohawk Street
Cohoes, NY 12047
(518) 235–3645
Manufactures pillow inserts, bed pillows, comforters, and bulk fiber.

Vista Window Film
4210 The Great Road
Fieldale, VA 24089
(800) 345–6088
Manufactures protective window film.

Sales Manual

An organized sales manual will make your appointment run smoother, because you will know exactly where to find the formula or price chart that you are looking for. All you will need for your manual is a large three-ring binder, some transparent paper covers, section separators, and a three-hole punch. Start by dividing the binder in sections. You'll have one for window coverings, subdivided into hard-lines and soft treatments. Another section will hold your bedding ensemble and accessories information. The other sections will hold the flooring information, upholstery charts, and wallpaper information.

Next you will need to sort through the price charts that your manufacturers have given you. Separate them into piles according to the binder dividers you have already completed. Copy the charts and formulas from this book as well as any others you have collected and add them accordingly to your sorted stacks. Punch holes in all the paperwork and place them in the proper sections of your binder.

You already should have negotiated the discounts with your manufacturer and arrived at your retail selling price for each of the products. Prepare a separate list for each section with your retail selling prices. There will be clients who will ask you to negotiate your prices, so include your high and low range so you will be prepared to negotiate.

Include any measuring instructions you may need. Before long you will be able to measure a standard job with your eyes closed, but it's always nice to be able to confirm the measurement requirements for odd-shaped windows and rooms, so include those instructions in your notebook. (These will be included with the price lists you get from each manufacturer.)

Finally, add any pictures that will help you express your ideas to clients more easily. It's not a good idea to include your entire portfolio in this binder because you will constantly be referring to it during an appointment; I've always carried doubles of my most commonly used pictures to have them handy.

Practice Worksheets

On the following pages there are sample price lists and practice problems. Use these to get familiar with the bidding process for each of the products. The answer key is located in the appendix of this book.

Practice Problems

Discounts

Your manufacturer discounts for the purposes of these exercises are as follows:

1. Miniblinds   50/50/40
2. Cellular Shades   50/50/25
3. Vertical Blinds   50/50/30
4. Drapery and Upholstery Fabrics   Less 50
5. Wallpaper   50/10

    Carpet, tile, and vinyl are priced at wholesale prices.

QUESTIONS

1. A customer has windows that measure as follows:

    > (three) $26\frac{1}{8}$" x $69\frac{7}{8}$"
    > (seven) 45" x 90"
    > (one) $11\frac{1}{2}$" x 72"

    The customer wants to put miniblinds in the windows. What is your cost?

2. Figure the price for a cellular shade that measures 43 by 68 inches. What would the price difference be if the shade came as two on one headrail?

3. Figure the price of an arch cellular shade that measures 30 by 15 inches.

4. Figure the price of a miniblind that measures 32 by 64 inches. What would the price difference be if the customer wanted the controls on the left side instead of the standard right side?

5. A customer has a window with a fabulous view. She wants a cellular shade that operates from the bottom up so she can enjoy privacy without losing the view. The window measures 36 by 60 inches. How much is your cost?

Miniblind Retail Price Chart

Length up to:	Width to: 23"	26"	29"	32"	36"	41"	45"	48"	54"
54"	$125	135	146	155	164	173	184	195	215
61"	$136	147	158	169	178	189	199	211	223
68"	$144	155	164	173	182	193	210	224	236
71"	$150	161	170	181	193	209	222	231	241
78"	$161	172	183	191	207	220	231	242	253
84"	$173	182	193	205	226	237	248	257	268
91"	$189	198	213	221	233	244	256	267	278
97"	$199	211	225	234	244	255	267	278	289
103"	$210	221	233	242	251	263	275	286	297

Note: For two or three blinds on one headrail, add a $145 surcharge. For blinds under 12", add a $40 surcharge. No charge for alternate control locations.

Cellular Shade Retail Price Chart

Length up to:	Width to: 24"	30"	36"	43"
36"	$78	96	114	121
41"	$90	107	125	133
48"	$100	116	130	142
54"	$112	127	141	154
61"	$123	138	154	166
68"	$136	149	167	178

Note: For bottom-up/top-down shade, add a 50 percent surcharge. For arch-top shade, add a $55 surcharge. For skylight shade, add a $130 surcharge. For two or three shades on one headrail, add a $50 surcharge.

Vertical Blind Retail Price Chart

Length up to:	Width to: 26"	38"	52"	64"	76"	84"	89"	100"
60"	$210	290	366	450	515	577	599	632
Insert	180	236	296	334	389	431	451	487
73"	240	326	414	489	571	632	659	741
Insert	191	251	318	361	420	458	470	538
84"	260	356	452	535	627	702	723	810
Insert	220	370	331	374	439	489	510	571

Drapery and Upholstery Fabric Retail Price Chart

Pattern	Price per yard	Uses	Content	Width
Spring	$26.90	Drapery	50/50 Poly/Cotton	48"
Summer	$27.10	Drapery	100% Cotton	54"
Autumn	$37.20	Upholstery	100% Cotton	54"
Winter	$47.45	Upholstery	100% Cotton	54"

Wallpaper Retail Price Chart

Pattern	Price per Single Roll
Plaid	$15.75
Stripe	$16.25
Floral	$17.10
Check	$19.00
Border	$11.99

Note: Wallpaper must be ordered in double rolls. Borders may be ordered in single rolls.

Carpet and Vinyl Wholesale Price List

Name	Price per Square Yard	Style
Contempo	$8.99	Carpet
Adobe	$9.50	Carpet
Country	$11.99	Vinyl
Eclectic	$13.98	Vinyl

Tile Wholesale Price List

Style	Price per Square Foot
Gloss	$1.20
Matte	$1.57
Stone	$1.99
Textured	$2.98

Note: Tile must be purchased in 45-square-foot boxes.

6. A customer wants to put a miniblind on an extremely large window. The window panes are broken up into three sections. The window measures 54 by 103 inches. What is the best application for this window?

7. A customer has a sliding glass door that he wants to put vertical blinds on. The measurement is 75 by 84 inches. The customer has a severe sun problem. What is the best application and how much is your cost?

8. You are figuring your cost for upholstering a customer's sofa. The sofa measures 78 inches long. Use the fabric Winter. You know that your labor cost is $250. What is your total cost? (*Hint:* Use the upholstery chart on page 187.)

9. What is your cost on a cornice board made out of the fabric Summer? (It is a solid.) Your labor cost is $10.00 per linear foot. Your installation charge is $3.00 per linear foot, and your lining cost is $4.00 per yard.

10. What is your cost for a swag and cascade treatment made out of the fabric Winter on a window that measures 75 inches? How many swags should you use? Your cascades measure 36 inches in length and are contrast-lined with the fabric Summer. Your workroom labor is $20.00 per linear foot, your installation charge is $3.00 per linear foot, and your lining cost is $4.00 per yard.

11. What is your cost for a pinch-pleat drapery that measures 40 by 84 inches? Use the fabric Autumn with a lining that costs $4.00 per yard. Your workroom charges $7.50 per width. Your installer charges $3.75 per linear foot. Your drapery hardware will cost $54.70.

12. You are designing an entire bedroom. Figure the price for a king-size throw bedspread that uses the fabric Summer. The workroom labor is $180. Also figure the price of the fabric for two corded pillow shams that measure 34 by 18 inches out of the fabric Spring. Figure out how much the fabric would cost to add three 12-inch round pillows with a dust ruffle in the fabric Fall.

13. You have measured a house for carpet and tile. The measurement for the room in which the carpet is to be installed is 12 by 15 feet. The measurement for the

room in which the tile is to be installed is 10 by 12 feet. The customer has selected Adobe for the carpet and Stone for the tile. Your cost for the pad is $2.00 per yard. Your installer charges $4.00 per yard for the carpet and $40.00 per hour for the tile (the job will take about three hours). What is your total cost?

14. What is your cost to wallpaper a room that measures 18 by 20 feet with 8-foot ceilings using the pattern Stripe? The customer also wants to add a border all the way around the room. How many rolls should you order?

Summary

This chapter isn't meant to be your only training in the design business. I have covered the very basic rules of the products. Ask your manufacturer's representative for more detailed training. Take a course. Read more books. Do everything that you can to ensure your confidence and success before you walk into your first appointment. Be sure you know what you're doing before you take on a design project.

Chapter Ten

Managing the Growth of Your Business

There comes a time in every business when the owner starts to realize that he or she needs help. This is the time when you will need to step back and analyze your business situation. Think of this stage as a fork in the road; the route you decide to take will forever impact your life and business. Sound scary? It can be if you're not prepared for it. You should have some idea when you start your business about how large you want it to become. At some point you will have to decide whether you want to stay a small, one-person operation or continue to grow into a larger, more profitable business, taking into account the effect on your home life.

It is possible in this type of business to have a few employees while still working out of your home. You are not likely, however (although anything is possible), to cultivate a large number of builder accounts while operating out of your home. If that is your goal, part of your long-term plan should be to move into a retail or office space because most builders require that you work out of a retail showroom. If your main goal is residential, you have more flexibility. Since most of your contact with customers will be in their home, your employees won't need a retail space to work out of either.

Moving Out

Operating a home-based business has more advantages than one can count, such as: no commute to and from an office, decreased need for wardrobe, a feeling of independence, and so on. But there comes a time in most businesses when the owner has to decide

Checklist

	Yes	No
You have too many employees to work comfortably.	___	___
You're running into zoning problems (i.e., too many cars come and go).	___	___
You have a shot at a builder account, but they want you to have an office.	___	___
You've simply outgrown your space.	___	___
Your work is interfering with your family life, or vice versa.	___	___

whether or not to move the business to an office or retail location. Below is a small check-list. If at any time in the course of your business you can answer yes to even one of these questions, you may want to consider moving out.

1. If you are beginning to feel as if you need more time, one of the first ways you can free up some of your time is to have someone else take over your books.

2. Once you have enough business, you can start converting contract laborers into full-time employees. You will have to do your individual numbers, but you should save money and time by paying the contractors a set fee or salary.

3. You may want to hire a part-time assistant to help you with the phones, order-ing, scheduling, and maintenance of the samples. Hiring someone who works even four hours a day will help.

4. The next person you will want to bring in is another designer. This can be tricky. You have two options. You can hire an experienced designer who requires no training, or you can hire an inexperienced person whom you will train to do things your way (more about this later).

5. If you have four or more designers working for you, you may need to hire a sales manager (or promote one of your designers and hire a new one). The sales man-ager can sell a limited number of jobs while taking care of the everyday business tasks.

Finding Good Employees

Perhaps one of the most challenging aspects of hiring employees is finding good, qualified people to fill the positions. As a business owner, your goal will be to get the best results for the smallest amount of advertising dollars spent. The way that you advertise for prospective employees will largely depend on where you live. If you live in a small to midsize city, you can run an effective newspaper ad for as long as it takes to find the perfect employee without having to spend a lot of money. But if you live in a large city, classified rates can be astronomical. You may choose to run an ad for one or two weeks in the classified section in addition to a few less traditional, less costly means to achieve your goal. Before I discuss the alternate ways to advertise for employees, let's take a look at a classified ad and what it should do for you.

If you are advertising for a bookkeeper or a secretary, the ad should be very straightforward and to the point. It might read something like this:

> *Part-time help needed for small business. Duties will include answering phone, filing, ordering materials, and scheduling. Will train. Possibility for advancement in the future. Call 777–7777.*

When you advertise for designers, the ad will need to be a little more creative. You will want to outline the importance of professionalism while highlighting the creative aspects of the job. You might use the following ad if you are advertising for an inexperienced designer.

> *Are You Good With Color? Small design firm now hiring designer. Must have desire to learn and succeed. Position requires attention to detail and sales ability. Will train the right person. 777–7777.*

Here are a few other ways to attract potential employees:

- *Ask your friends and family.* This technique can be especially useful if you are hiring an inexperienced designer. (Everybody knows someone who wants to be a designer.) You will need to make it clear that although you plan on hiring the best person for the job, you will certainly appreciate any referrals that they give you.

- *Go to your local design school.* Most design schools require that their students do an internship at a design firm. The internships last from a couple of weeks to a few months. Every school has different requirements, so call the one in your area. If you find someone with whom you work well, you have the option of extending the internship and offering the person a full-time job.
- *Ask your manufacturers' representatives and contractors.* The fact that people in this business talk to one another can work to your advantage. Get out the word that you are hiring. Ask your reps to let you know if they hear of someone who wants to change jobs.

The Interview Process

Think back to the times when you've been interviewed by a potential employer. You were probably nervous, and it was generally the circumstances of the interview that made the difference in whether or not you felt it was successful. If an employer were interviewing for an accounting position, the interview would be a lot more straightforward than if the interview were for a designer position. As the employer, it will be up to you to set the stage.

Before you conduct your first interview, you should make a list of the traits you are looking for. For instance, if you are interviewing for a designer position, the following traits may apply: outgoing personality, good with people, trustworthy, good with details, fast thinker, professional dresser, responsible, confident.

Form your interview questions around the traits that you desire. If you are looking for an experienced designer, you will need to throw in specific questions about product and technique. If you have narrowed the selection down to a few good people, you might want to give them a test, such as the one in the products chapter, to determine how much they really know.

The Group Interview

There is a new trend emerging: the group interview. This may be the best way to spot the most qualified salespeople in your hiring pool. Simply invite a group of applicants to take part in a group interview, informing them beforehand. After they arrive, have them take a quiz on product knowledge, and then ask them to sit in a circle of chairs. Then throw out questions to get the group talking, such as: "What's the best way to build rapport with a customer?" or "Who can tell me why it's important to up-sell?" The natural leaders will stand out, and you'll get to observe how each applicant operates under pressure. At the end of the interview, ask the applicants whom you're interested in back for a private interview.

Probationary Period

It's a good idea to hire someone with the understanding that it's on a probation basis. If you are hiring an experienced applicant, a three-month probation period should be enough time to establish whether or not he or she will work out. If you are training someone, six months is a reasonable amount of time. Remember, it costs money every time you hire and train an employee, so you will want to give the new person every chance possible to succeed at the job.

Noncompete Agreements

There were times in the early stages of my business when I felt like a finishing school for designers. Over and over again I would hire new designers, train them, and equip them with samples, only to be left in the dust when they would leave and start their own business.

The best way to avoid this is to use noncompete agreements. The agreement should be drawn up by an attorney and signed on the first day of employment along with the application and tax forms. The agreement protects you against a designer who would use you for training, become friendly with your customers, and then leave to start his or her own business, taking some of your clients along. By signing the agreement, designers promise not to go into a competing business (for themselves or for one of your competitors) for a predetermined amount of time. It also sets guidelines for after the time is up. It will restrict how geographically close to your business they can open theirs. In order for this agreement to hold up in court, the restrictions must be reasonable, so make sure your attorney is experienced with this aspect of the law.

What to Pay

If you are hiring a bookkeeper, office help, or contractor, you will have to pay the going rates in your area. It's simple enough to determine the rates—just look in the paper to see what other companies are offering. Try to hire the best possible candidate for what you can afford. When it's time to hire designers, you have a few more options. You can pay a designer one of three ways: salary, commission, or salary plus commission.

Salary

Paying a designer a salary with no commission is detrimental to that person's sales, thereby negatively affecting your bottom line. Part of a designer's job is to upgrade products and sell the customer add-ons, such as pillows or upholstery, to increase the price of the job. Without commission incentive, she or he won't be as inclined to sell as much.

Commission Only

For a small business, this is the most affordable way to hire employees. You should pay the designer 10 to 15 percent of his or her gross sales. Let's say that you offered the designer a straight 10 percent commission. The designer would have to sell $15,000 per month to make $1,500 per month in commission, which totals $18,000 per year. In order to afford this, you should have enough business to support yourself, your business, and the new employee. Since part of the new designer's job will be to bring you additional business, the earning potential is limitless.

Salary Plus Commission

Let's imagine that you still plan to offer the new designer 10 percent of her or his gross sales as an incentive. You might offer a $1,500 guaranteed salary plus 10 percent commission on any amount over $15,000 in sales. You would be paying the same amount as in the commission-only example except that the first $1,500 would be guaranteed regardless of whether the designer sold $15,000. (If you don't have at least $15,000 per month in excess business, you're not ready to hire a designer.)

Quotas

In order to keep specific goals in mind, you can set up quotas for your designers. If when you hire them you have $10,000 in excess sales, set a quota for $12,000 for their second month. Once they accomplish that, set a higher quota for the next month. It's a good idea to reward them when they achieve their goals. Besides the obvious reward of the additional commission that they will be making, offer them something else, such as dinner for two at a nice restaurant if they make the quota that month.

Yet another way to motivate your employees is to offer them a bonus for harder-to-reach goals. You can have two quota systems set up. For instance, if your employees' quota is $15,000 per month, you can set an optional advanced quota of $22,000. If they reach this higher goal, they will be rewarded with a 15 percent commission on everything over and above the first $15,000. (This would mean that instead of making $2,200 that month, their salary would be $2,550.) The harder goal motivated them to sell more, and you earned a profit on the $7,000 in increased sales.

Gas Allowance

Some design firms offer to pay for their designer's gas. Because of the nature of the business, it's not unusual for a designer to use two tanks of gas per week. If you want to reimburse your employees, simply ask them to keep a mileage log and turn in receipts for gas used at work. This little step will go a long way in employee satisfaction.

Keeping Designers Motivated

As in every sales job, it's easy to get frustrated and feel unappreciated. I have found that a little encouragement goes a long way in keeping most designers motivated. I remember the time when one of my designers signed a large job. Everyone in the office knew how long and hard she had been working in trying to land this job. When she finally did get the client to sign the contract, I threw a little congratulations party. I spent about $60 on champagne and food, but the loyalty I gained from that employee was invaluable.

Another easy way to motivate your employees is to include them in the manufacturers' *spiffs* (promotional contests). They will give you $5.00 (or another specified amount) for every product sold from a particular line. It can be beneficial for you to pass this incentive along to your employees. If they know that they will make $5.00 for every wood blind that they sell, they will be more apt to upgrade a lot more miniblind sales to wood blind sales (which also will put more money in *your* pocket because wood blinds sell for more money than miniblinds).

Hiring a Sales Manager

I won't spend a lot of time on this topic because this is a book about home-based business. But if you want to become a large home-based business with numerous designers, you may need a manager. If you decide to hire at least four designers, I suggest that you hire a sales manger to supervise them. She or he can handle the day-to-day operations and take over any responsibilities that a part-time office helper would do, such as ordering materials and scheduling appointments and installations. The sales manager can even sell a few jobs when there's time. You can pay the manager a small salary, with an override on the total gross sales. Thus part of the manager's responsibility will be to increase your sales. He or she will do so by keeping the designers motivated and by personally marketing builders and large accounts. You must be ambitious and willing to work a lot of hours in order to accomplish this level of business, but it can be done.

Training Your Employees

Training your employees is vital to their success as well as the success of your business. The more training your employees have, the better they will perform their job. Training instills confidence, and confidence translates into increased sales.

Ask your manufacturers' representatives to give your employees in-depth training on their products. If you ask each representative to do this, your employee will be well on the way to an overall understanding of all the products. Send your employees to seminars that are held by the various manufacturers and trade associations. Most manufacturers will hold free seminars that introduce new products (or simply go over the old ones) at least once a year. Most trade associations offer classes and give the designers certification awards for completing them. There is usually a fee for these classes, but they are well worth the expense.

Encourage your designers to take classes in design. You may even want to consider reimbursing them for half or even all of the tuition costs. Remember, the better trained and supported they are, the more they will sell and fewer costly mistakes will be made.

You Can Do It!

I hope I have been successful in teaching you the basics of the home-based interior design business. This business is one of the few that can be started on a limited budget and still have the enormous growth potential that it does. I can still remember the feeling I had once I made the decision to go out on my own and earn my own way. It was truly freeing. I wish you all the success in the world, and I hope that your experience with the design world will be as gratifying as mine has been. Good luck and God bless.

Appendix

Trade Publications

Listed below are some trade publications I have found useful. You can also ask your manufacturers' representatives for the names and addresses of others. It is possible that they may be able to get you a subscription for free.

Periodicals

Drapery and Window Coverings
P.O. Box 13079
North Palm Beach, FL 33408-7079

Window Fashion, Design and Education
  Magazine
4225 White Bear Parkway
Suite 400
St. Paul, MN 55110

Flooring Magazine
114 Elkton Lane
North Babylon, NY 11703

Western Floors
22801 Ventura Boulevard
Woodland Hills, CA 91364

Books you should own

The Encyclopedia of Window Fashions
Randall International
P.O. Box 1656
Orange, CA 92668

Drapery workrooms use this as a standard for window treatments. Buy it!

Hard Window Coverings Made Easy
10299 Scripps Trail
Suite 103
San Diego, CA 92131

An in-depth guide to the hard-line window covering products.

Sales Master Training Program
  by DuPont
DuPont flooring systems division
Walnut Run Building
Wilmington, DE 19880

A self-help training guide to flooring products (given to DuPont customers).

Associations

American Society of Interior
  Designers (ASID)
608 Massachusetts Avenue NE
Washington, D.C. 20002
(202) 546–3480

The Carpet & Rug Institute
P.O. Box 2048
Dalton, GA 30722
(800) 882–8846

A good source for educational and technical information.

Color Association of the United States
409 West Forty-fourth Street
New York, NY 10036
(212) 582–6884

Produces an annual report that forecasts upcoming colors for most interior design products.

Decorative Window Coverings
  Associations (DWCA)
1050 North Lindberg Boulevard
Saint Louis, MO 63132-2994
(314) 991–3470

Sponsors seminars and meetings about the window covering industry. The association consists of manufacturers and distributors that help to educate the retail-level person.

DraperyPro
1025 Lake Street
Huntington Beach, CA 92648–3529
www.draperypro.com

A national networking group that concentrates on the issues of soft window coverings.

Home Fashion Information Network
557 South Duncan
Clearwater, FL 34616
(800) 275–1891

A good source for information relating to the wall covering industry.

National Association of Home-Based
  Businesses
NAHBB, Inc.
10451 Mill Run Circle, Suite 400
Owings Mills, MA 21117
(410) 363–3698
www.usahomebusiness.com

Organization will analyze your business plan and give advice.

Answers to the practice questions on pages 185–90

1. $327.60. See the surcharge for shades under 12".

2. $33.38 for the regular priced shade. $42.75 for two shades on one headrail. See the surcharge listed at the bottom of the price chart and add it to the retail before you deduct your discounts.

3. $28.31. Again, remember to figure in your surcharge.

4. $25.95. No additonal charge for controls change. See note at bottom of price chart.

5. $43.31. Add a 50 percent surcharge for a bottom-up shade. See note on price chart.

6. The best application for this window is to use three miniblinds on one headrail. Remember, there is a $145 surcharge for this feature.

7. $109.73. To increase energy efficiency, use insert channels on the vertical blinds.

8. $605.95.

9. $157.75.

10. $471.04.

11. $370.90.

12. King-size throw $342.60. Fabric for the shams $53.80. The pillows will cost you $35.60.

13. The carpet will cost $270 and the tile will cost $358.80.

14. The wallpaper will cost $146.20 and you will need six border rolls (remember to round up).

Index

T

V

W

About the Author

Suzanne DeWalt started her own home-based interior design business in 1988, successfully growing and expanding the business to include five designers and a full-time installation crew. Before starting her business, she worked as a representative for a carpet, window covering, and fabric manufacturer.

Suzanne has also published numerous articles on home-based and small businesses in *Home Business Magazine*, *Wealth Building*, and *Window Fashions Magazine*. She now lives in Texas with her son and devotes her professional time to writing.